Worshiping God is our primary calling and greatest honor. In *Next Wave*, Bob Sorge paints a clear picture of the new ways God will be moving through the ministry of worship in this next season. His history with the worship movement brings understanding to the powerful prophetic insights he shares in each chapter. I absolutely love this book and encourage everyone to read it!

BILL JOHNSON
Bethel Church, Redding, CA
Author of *Born for Significance* and
Hope in Any Crisis

Next Wave is absolutely outstanding! How can I express its impact on me? I'm requiring all my leaders to read it. This message is inspired by the Holy Spirit and gives us hope for the future. May this book spread throughout the Church and awaken us to the true purpose of worship: His Presence.

KAREN WHEATON
Founder and Senior Leader
The RAMP, Hamilton, AL

God has given my friend Bob Sorge an invaluable voice to the Body of Christ, and I'm so glad he's written this book. You're going to be inspired by his insight into where God is taking today's worship movement. Get ready to catch the *Next Wave* of the Holy Spirit's movements in the earth!

WILLIAM McDOWELL
Lead Pastor, Deeper Fellowship Church, Orlando, FL
Grammy Award-nominated Worship
Leader and Songwriter

Bob Sorge has helped shape the modern-day worship and prayer movement. His teachings and resources have brought a voice of clarity and conviction to our worship leaders and musicians through the years. In *Next Wave*, he helps us understand how the past moves of God have been preparing us for what's coming. I'm deeply grateful for Bob's ministry and its profound impact upon UPPERROOM.

MICHAEL MILLER
Lead Pastor, UPPERROOM Dallas

The Lord has enabled Bob Sorge to equip and inspire leaders for such a time as this. This book will help you process the uncertainties of our past season and ignite fresh expectation for the *Next Wave* that's coming.

DANTE BOWE
Artist and Songwriter, Bethel Music

Unlike anyone I've known, Bob has a singular heart for worship and its value to the Bride of Christ. With in-depth insight on the temperature and culture of worship in the Church, Bob engages us in a necessary conversation: That no matter how our world changes around us, we must use the great weapon of praise and always be ready to capture the *Next Wave* of the Spirit.

RITA SPRINGER
Single mom and lover of Jesus

Bob Sorge's voice to the worship community through the years has been invaluable. In *Next Wave,* he leads us brilliantly through an insightful synopsis of worship in the Church over the past sixty years, and then provides a bold vision for where worship is going in the Body of Christ. This is a must-read for all worship leaders.

CALEB CULVER
Co-Author, *Reckless Love*

Bob is a father, mentor, and friend. His writings have inspired and equipped me personally, and now with *Next Wave* he provides fresh insight on worship that is timely and revelatory. You're about to be better equipped to follow Christ and lead others in our hurting world. Everyone needs to get a copy and read it!

JEFF DEYO
Professor, North Central University
Author, *SPARK: A Comprehensive Handbook on Worship Leadership*

What Bob has written has deeply shaken my spirit. He's calling today's generation of worshipers to plumb the depths of God's Presence and pursue greater Glory. It's time to seek a reality in God that will catapult us into greater lovesick devotion to Jesus and His Kingdom.

JAKE STEMO
Presence Worship
Wichita, KS

NEXT WAVE

NEXT WAVE

WORSHIP IN A NEW ERA

BOB SORGE

DESTINY IMAGE® PUBLISHERS, INC.
P.O. Box 310, Shippensburg, PA 17257-0310
"Promoting Inspired Lives."

This book and all other Destiny Image and Destiny Image Fiction books are available at Christian bookstores and distributors worldwide.

Cover design by Eileen Rockwell
Interior design by Terry Clifton

For more information on foreign distributors, call 717-532-3040.
Reach us on the Internet: www.destinyimage.com.

ISBN 13 TP: 978-0-7684-5878-7
ISBN 13 eBook: 978-0-7684-5879-4
ISBN 13 HC: 978-0-7684-5881-7
ISBN 13 LP: 978-0-7684-5880-0

For Worldwide Distribution, Printed in the U.S.A.
1 2 3 4 5 6 7 8 / 25 24 23 22 21

ACKNOWLEDGMENTS

As I prepared to write this book, I solicited insights and opinions from some of my friends. As we prayed and pondered together, their feedback and input about where God is taking us in worship was valuable and helpful. I'm very grateful for how eagerly and willingly the following friends engaged with me on this topic: Caleb Culver, Tim Fortin, Chris Abke, Diatra Langford, Chris DuPre, Clayton Brooks, David Forlu, David Lugo, Dick Grout, Jaye Thomas, Katie Reed, Laura Souguellis, Mary Alessi, Rita Springer, Emma Hawthorne, Jake Stemo, Alan Goke, Matthew Penner, Chris Tofilon, Justin Rizzo, Will Riddle, Zac Dinsmore, Brenton Dowdy, Mark Hendrickson, J.D. King, Josh Sullivan, Drew Smith, and Ruben Cervantes.

I'm so grateful to God for these, and for all my friends in the worshiping community of Christ, who are reaching with me for the greatest waves of the Holy Spirit history has seen.

ACKNOWLEDGEMENTS

Contents

Chapter 1

Where Is God Taking Us in Worship?

THAT'S THE QUESTION I'm tackling in this book. A *lot* of people are wanting to know the answer to that question!

Get ready to be surprised.

The global shockwaves that began in 2020 have awakened us to the realization that our world will never return to what it was. The rate of global change is accelerating. It's a new era for virtually everything—worship and church included.

I watched in astonishment in 2020 as the doors of churches literally around the world were closed due to the coronavirus pandemic. The Lord's words in Malachi 1:10 came to mind,

> *"Who is there even among you who would shut the doors, so that you would not kindle fire on My*

altar in vain? I have no pleasure in you," says the Lord of hosts, "Nor will I accept an offering from your hands."

God had shut our doors, and I couldn't help but ask, "Lord, is there something about our worship that You're wanting to address?"

Many churches took their worship services online, and leaders were grateful we had this option available to us. It meant our services could reach people in spaces we would have never reached—a marvelous benefit.

How effective are online church services? Well, when it comes to sermons, they can impact an online audience in powerful ways. But when it comes to worship, it's different. Online worship is just not the same as in-person worship. Sometimes it feels distant, sterile, non-engaging, or flat.

No area of local church life has been more deeply impacted by the pandemic than corporate worship.

Where is it going to go from here?

When we pan back for a bird's-eye view, we're struck by how significantly the corporate worship expressions of the Church have changed over the past sixty years. The changes are stunning, remarkable, almost cataclysmic. Never has the Church's worship seen such enormous changes in so brief a period of time.

We're being carried along in an epic drama that's bigger than all of us, and we're eager to know where it's going.

I believe God is preparing the Church for a new wave of Holy Spirit visitation. All flesh is going to see the glory of God together, and a worldwide harvest of souls will be brought into the Kingdom (see Isa. 40:5; Joel 2:28; Matt. 24:14; Rom. 11:12–15). It will be like a latter rain harvest (see James 5:7).

As these waves crash on the shores of the Church, how will they affect our worship? I invite you to walk with me through this book; let's peer into this question together. God wants us to catch a vision for where He's taking us because, when we see it (even if just partially), we can cooperate with His grace and press toward the prize.

Based on hints I see in God's Word, I'm going to lay out several indicators of where I believe we're going. But before we look ahead, we must first look back. Why? Because we can't fully understand where we're going until we appreciate where we've come from. Yesterday positions us for tomorrow.

At the release of this book, I'm sixty-four years old (born in 1957). I was raised in a pastor's home, first in western Canada and then upstate New York, and in one sense literally grew up in church. I've been watching the Church worship all my life, which means I've had a front-row seat to the changes that have taken place in worship over the past sixty years. I want to launch this book by describing those changes as I experienced them personally.

Now, I realize that my window on the past sixty years is very subjective and narrow, and there are parts of the world where worship has been expressed very differently—such as in Africa and Asia, for example. The experience of some readers will have been very different from mine. But all I can do is speak from my own personal background. I'm going to describe how worship has changed—as I've watched it in North America—over the past sixty years.

We're going to start by doing a survey of worship through the past six decades. Why would such a survey be helpful? Because:

1. History has always served as an example to help us chart our way forward (see 1 Cor. 10:6).

2. Many of today's worshipers, especially among the youth, aren't aware of how worship has developed and changed over the past sixty years. Most readers simply haven't spent that many years in the Church. I think you're going to find the following historical sketch both interesting and illuminating.

3. There are dynamics about yesterday's worship that will mark and characterize tomorrow's worship. I'll do my best to help you see that.

Therefore, I urge you to read this book in order, rather than leafing ahead to the end of the book. You'll understand and appreciate our conclusions much better if you'll walk through all the chapters sequentially. Plus, you're going to enjoy the story!

So let's go there. Come with me as I describe what corporate worship was like from as far back as my childhood. We're going to start with the 1960s.

(Group Study Questions appear in this manner at the end of each chapter. Take your small group through this book together!)

Questions for Wave Riders:

1. What are some of the ways coronavirus has impacted worship at the local church level?

2. As you look ahead at the coming decades, where do you see the Lord taking the Body of Christ in worship? Discuss this in your group.

Chapter 2

WORSHIP IN THE 1960s

BACK IN THE 1960s, many churches had just one instrument on their platform—a piano. Some churches had both a piano and organ, and often these instruments sat on opposite sides of the platform. (Guitars were rare in churches in those days.) Many churches were fortunate if they had someone to play either instrument, and few had more than two musicians during worship.

My mother was an exceptional gospel hymn musician, extremely versatile on both piano and organ, and was the coveted musician for conferences and camp meetings in our region. She handed to her two sons her flair for playing gospel-style piano.

One day she announced to me, "You're playing piano in church from now on."

I immediately complained, "I don't know how to play piano," but that was of no consequence to her.

It was useless to try to argue with my mom, so the following Sunday I sat at the piano, and she took the helm at the organ. She just put the organ volume pedal to the metal and rammed every song through. I sat at the piano on the opposite side of the platform and played catch-up through the entire worship service. I was so mortified by my embarrassing performance that I went home and started practicing piano like crazy. The truth is I learned to play piano in church alongside my mom.

In those days, we had *song services*. And the singing was led by a *song leader*. In our church tradition, the song leader was usually one of the deacons. If you were voted by the congregation to serve as a deacon for a term, that meant you would automatically take your turn as the song leader every few weeks. Musical abilities weren't necessary. All the song leader really needed to do was announce the hymn numbers. "Let's start with hymn number 79, and we'll sing verses one, two, and four." From there, the piano or organ would take it away.

In the 1960s, almost all "non-liturgical" churches had the same general worship experience. Whether the name on the door was Pentecostal, Holiness, Baptist, Nazarene, Christian & Missionary Alliance, African Methodist Episcopal, Salvation Army, Wesleyan, Evangelical Free, Brethren, Mennonite, or something similar, all the churches sang four hymns.

What was a hymn? A song with two or more verses and a chorus. Hymns were printed in songbooks called *hymnals*. Hymnals were usually rather thick, with a copy provided for each person in the congregation. All the hymns were numbered, and it was the song leader's job to call out the number of the next hymn to be sung, as well as the verses that would be sung.

After the first hymn was sung, the song leader would announce, "Turn now to hymn number 234, and we'll sing verses one, two, and four." After the second hymn was sung, the third hymn would be introduced. At the conclusion of the third hymn, a fourth hymn would be announced. "Turn to hymn number 606." After the fourth hymn, everyone was seated, and it was typically time for the announcements, or offering, or special music.

Here's an example of a hymn that was very commonly sung in the 1960s:

Blessed Assurance

Verse 1

Blessed assurance, Jesus is mine;
Oh, what a foretaste of glory divine!
Heir of salvation, purchase of God,
Born of His Spirit, washed in His blood.

Chorus

This is my story, this is my song,

Praising my Savior all the day long.

This is my story, this is my song,

Praising my Savior all the day long.

Four hymns such as this were sung in churches during the song service, almost regardless of the church name (except for historic churches such as Roman Catholic, Lutheran, Episcopal, etc.).

I was raised in a Pentecostal church tradition. In our church, we sang four hymns, but then we had one feature that was unique from most churches: We also sang *choruses*.

What was a chorus? Basically, a hymn with no verses. After singing four hymns, we would close with a chorus which was usually more contemporary in composition and was often sung with spirited enthusiasm.

To give you a feel for the choruses we sang, here are some of the chorus titles popular in our church in the 1960s—you may even recognize one of these songs:

- "Turn Your Eyes upon Jesus" (Helen Howarth Lemmel, 1922)
- "Oh, the Blood of Jesus, It Washes White as Snow" (unknown)
- "I Have Decided to Follow Jesus" (Sadhu Sundar Singh)
- "Spirit of the Living God, Fall Fresh on Me" (Daniel Iverson, 1926)

Four hymns and a chorus—that was Sunday morning worship in my church tradition in the 1960s. Now, let's look at the 1970s.

Questions for Wave Riders:

1. What hymn has special meaning to you? Do you have a story about it to tell the group?

2. How would you define the difference between a song leader and a worship leader?

3. Are there any choruses you know from yesteryear that you wish would make a comeback today?

Chapter 3

WORSHIP IN THE 1970S

THE 1970S SAW the era of the overhead projector. Around 1970, Scripture choruses began to proliferate, and since they weren't printed in any of the hymnals, the churches were looking for a way to get the lyrics in front of the people so they could sing along. The solution? Project the words onto a screen or wall with an overhead projector. That tool helped Scripture choruses multiply globally.

The spread of Scripture songs was greatly helped by Calvary Chapel's Maranatha! Music. Founded in 1971 by Chuck Smith, the Maranatha singers recorded Scripture songs often sung in unison, and the recordings went around the world. My friend Karen Lafferty wrote "Seek Ye First," a popular Scripture song at that time. Also popular in the 1970s were the Scripture songs, "This Is the Day" and "I Will Enter His Gates."

The Jesus movement of the late 1960s, which saw a marvelous ingathering of souls among hippies, basically transitioned into what became known as the *Charismatic movement*. During the Charismatic movement, believers from virtually all denominations experienced a greater fullness of the Holy Spirit.

The most compelling distinctive of worship in the 1970s Charismatic movement was a practice that was called *singing in the Spirit* or *free worship*. Here's my story of the time I first experienced it.

The year was 1970, and I had just become a teenager. My family lived on the coast of British Columbia, Canada, and it was time for summer vacation. The Lord led us sovereignly to a family camp just north of Seattle called World M.A.P. (Ralph Mahoney, director). When we entered the meeting, it was as though we stepped into a different world. For the first time ever, I witnessed singing in the Spirit. Here's how it worked.

After a song was sung, the pianist would end the song on the I chord,[1] hold the chord with the sustain pedal, and the voices of the people would then take over. The people's singing might start off gently, but before long it became full-throated. It seemed like virtually *everyone* was lifting their voices to the Lord in their own personal praise, and the room would fill with sound. The piano or organ might support the singing with a sustained chord and some pleasant arpeggios, but the energy of the song came from the people, not the platform.

The basses would go low, the sopranos would go high, and across the spectrum of the human vocal range, spontaneous songs would lift to the Lord simultaneously. The people had found their voice, and the atmosphere was electric! God's Presence would sometimes be so strong in the house that we were unmistakably experiencing Psalm 22:3—God inhabiting the praises of His people. Occasionally, people would say they thought they heard angelic choirs singing with us.

The leaders on the platform didn't try to stir up or exhort the people to praise. They didn't have to because the Spirit was energizing the song in the people and no one could hold them back. The momentum of the crescendos felt something like the energy that must have carried the praises at Christ's triumphal entry.

When this *free worship* would arise, some people would sing their own song in English, and others would sing in other tongues (*glossolalia*). It would all rise in one glorious cloud of indistinguishable language, and no one paid much attention to the song of their neighbor because all eyes were fixed on Jesus.

The song would rise and fall, swell and abate, almost like the tides of the ocean or the breathing of a living creature. After a while, the singing would subside, and the room grow quiet—until suddenly someone's voice from somewhere in the room would lift in song, and the entire room would pick it up and soar again on the winds of the Spirit. In this manner, through cycles of increase and diminishment, singing in the Spirit on one sustained chord could go on for 15 minutes, 30 minutes, 45 minutes, or even an hour. The praise was unstoppable!

It was the song of the people.

Singing in the Spirit produced a great divide in the Body of Christ in the 1970s. Let me explain.

The churches split into two general groups: Those who practiced singing in the Spirit and those who didn't. The big point of contention? *Glossalalia*—which is the New Testament Greek word for speaking in other tongues as experienced widely in the early church (for examples, see Acts 2:2–4; 10:46; 19:6; 1 Cor. 12:10). Singing in the Spirit was associated implicitly with speaking in tongues, and since many churches didn't practice tongues, they had no interest in singing in the Spirit. Because of the *glosso-lalia* controversy, many churches chose not to participate in the Charismatic movement and its new expression of worship. Hence, the worshiping church divided into two groups.

How can I properly identify these two groups? Finding fitting language in the following discussion is very difficult. There was one group open to singing in the Spirit and speaking in tongues, and this group was comprised of some Pentecostal groups as well as Charismatics from a variety of church backgrounds. In the Charismatic movement, there were Charismatic Catholics, Lutherans,

Episcopalians, Presbyterians, Baptists, Methodists, and a host of other labels. When they experienced speaking in tongues in Charismatic gatherings, some believers left their churches because they were no longer welcome, and they found churches where speaking in tongues was accepted.

The second group included churches that didn't support speaking in tongues. These churches had no interest in participating in the Charismatic movement, and instead, they maintained their 1960s paradigm of singing. They might throw in a Scripture chorus, but for the most part they stayed with the four-hymn model.

For ease of communication in this book, I'm going to assign a label to each group. In doing so, I'm certain to irk some readers. I'm not meaning to offend. I'm meaning to be helpful by using language that communicates. There simply are no labels that are adequate and precise. I've considered labels such as evangelicals, historic churches, traditional versus non-traditional, liturgical versus non-liturgical, etc. None of the labels are adequate or perfect.

With that being said, what name shall we give to the group that accepted singing in the Spirit? For lack of a better term, I'm going to call those churches the *Charismatics*, even though that will upset some people. There are some Pentecostals, for example, that do not want to be called Charismatics, but yet they practice singing in the Spirit. The term *Charismatics* is a woefully inadequate term, but it's the best one I know to use for this discussion.

And then the group that *didn't* accept singing in the Spirit, what name shall we give to that group? This group represents a wide diversity of denominations, and for lack of a better term, I'm going to call this group the *Baptists*. I recognize that's not an adequate designation because most of the churches in this group are not actually Baptists. But for lack of a better appellation, I'm lumping together all the churches that didn't support speaking in tongues and calling them the *Baptist* group. Please over-look the weakness of my language.

There came a great divide in the 1970s between the Charismatics and the Baptists. The Charismatics moved into free worship and the singing of Scripture songs, while the Baptists stayed in their 1960s model of four hymns. It's difficult for some believers today to really appreci-ate just how extremely divisive the issue of tongues was in the Body of Christ back in the 1970s. The theological differences separated many Jesus-loving believers. Thus, the worship practices of the Church divided into two dif-ferent streams, and the two rivers would run parallel for the next thirty years.

Among the Charismatics, there was an explosion of Scripture songs and worship choruses. One of the block-buster songs of that decade was Pete Sanchez's 1975 song,

"I Exalt Thee." I still remember my first encounter with that song in 1975. The Lord's Presence was strong in the meeting, and the Holy Spirit's energy on that song was a captivating experience for me.

Another beloved song from that era was Laurie Klein's, "I Love You, Lord." Maranatha! Music helped that song go around the world.

Again, worship in the 1970s among the Charismatics was distinguished primarily by Scripture songs, free worship, and the transported song of the people.

Up next? Worship in the 1980s.

Questions for Wave Riders:

1. Have you ever experienced 1970s-style singing in the Spirit on a sustained I chord? What was the experience like for you?

2. How do you feel about *glossolalia*? Do you believe that speaking in other tongues is something to be coveted or downplayed?

3. Would you have enough confidence as a group to worship the Lord together in this small group meeting in I-chord free worship? Want to try it and see how the Holy Spirit might honor it?

Note

1. *I chord* is a term in music theory used to describe the chord built on the first note of the key at hand. So if a song is in the key of C, the I chord would be a C chord.

Chapter 4

WORSHIP IN THE 1980S

LET ME TELL the story of how I experienced worship in the 1980s.

In August of 1981, I was hired as the Music Director at Elim Bible Institute in Upstate New York. I was called *Music Director* because that was the term used most commonly in those days for the person who directed the musical and worship life of a local congregation. It would take several years for the term *worship leader* to come into common usage. I was stoked because this was my first full-time employment in music ministry.

As I examined the Bible Institute's music curriculum, the Lord gave me a desire to train worship leaders for ministry. At that time, the idea that a Bible school would train worship leaders was altogether novel. Nobody was doing it in 1981, and nobody was writing books to support that kind of curriculum. I bought every book I could find on music and worship ministry, but no books existed at the time that taught and equipped worship leaders. A few books helped equip music ministers on how to lead a choir and run a church music department, but those books were targeting churches that sang four hymns on Sundays, did a choir special during the offering, and performed musicals and pageants for special events such as Christmas. There was no literature for worship leaders, so I attempted to craft a curriculum based upon personal experience and the tidbits I could gather from an array of sources. My first year as an instructor was passionate but limping.

In the summer of 1982, I had a life-changing experience. I learned about a music conference happening in Detroit, and since I was desperate to glean in my capacity as a Bible school teacher, I decided to go. The event was called the *International Worship Symposium*, whose heritage came out of the Latter Rain Revival of 1948. When I stepped into the auditorium, I was stunned at what was happening before me.

A veritable symphony was on the platform, with musicians playing trumpets, trombones, violins, cellos, clarinets, French horns, etc. The meeting would commence with known songs or new songs, with much energy and passion in the room. And then, between songs, they would often flow into singing in the Spirit. The conference delegates would sing in the Spirit to one sustained chord as was typical for the 1970s, and the symphony would support them. But then they did something

I hadn't witnessed before: The entire symphony would begin to play a simple chord progression, over and over, and the worshipers would move spontaneously in song as their voices followed the changing chords. Thus, two elements were added to the sustained chord of the 1970s: rhythm and chord changes. It was the first time I experienced this, and I found the effect electrifying!

At times the rhythm was smooth and flowing, at other times militant and pulsating. Sometimes all the instruments would stop except for the rhythm section, and the worship would continue with just drums and congas, etc. In such moments, the worship often took on a militant feeling of spiritual warfare. Then the wind and stringed instruments would join again, and the melodies would soar.

Next a trumpeter would step up to a microphone and launch into a prophetic oracle on the trumpet while supported by the symphony. That only served to further ignite the fiery love in the hearts of the worshipers, and the congregation would take over again.

Then a singer would step forward and sing a prophetic oracle on a microphone. Often the oracle would extol the beauty and holiness of Christ or express the Lord's love for His people. All the oracles and sung responses were spontaneous songs of the moment. Those prophetic songs, whether sung or played, were like fire starters. After the prophetic solo, the gathering would erupt in new levels of fervency and love for Jesus.

When the symphony got on a chord progression, it provided the worshipers with musical and melodic variety. Everyone could sing their own song to the Lord, and melody lines could cover the range of the human voice, all being sung spontaneously and simultaneously. By adding rhythm and chord progressions to the 1970s model of free worship, the 1980s model provided for more interest, creativity, and sense of movement.

The 1982 Detroit conference was an encounter of spiritual awakening for me. I realized that a worship movement had launched, and I jumped in with both feet.

I organized and led my first worship conference at Elim Bible Institute in 1983. Similar conferences began to arise all over the nation, popcorn style. Almost immediately, other nations got on board, and worship conferences began to convene all over the world. The advent of worship conferences was a new phenomenon in the 1980s. Churches that were eager for fresh fire in their congregation would send their worship teams to these kinds of events, and they would return home with fresh vision and consecration.

At worship conferences, when I would teach on the concept of a worship leading team, people would pack the room to hear a workshop on such an idea. In the 1960s and 1970s, church musicians rarely rehearsed for Sunday worship; they just showed up and did it. The idea of a worship team rehearsing and laboring together for excellence in their ministry—that came together in the 1980s. Today, almost all churches have robust worship team ministries, but back in the 1980s it was a groundbreaking concept.

What I'm describing about 1980s worship—worship teams moving in free worship with rhythms and chord progressions—was present only among Charismatic churches. At the time, Baptist churches (and again, my two designations are woefully inadequate) were not open to it. Instead, they maintained their 1960s model of four hymns with perhaps a Scripture song.

Around the 80s, several groups began to publish worship music in cassette form. The Vineyard churches (under John Wimber) began to distribute the worship songs coming out of their movement. They were known for their emphasis on intimacy with Jesus, and their passion for Jesus infected the global Body of Christ. Hosanna's Integrity Music had their launch in the mid-80s, and quickly gathered momentum. Their content was more eclectic, drawing from a wide diversity of groups and nations in the Body of Christ. And they were also amazingly prolific, producing a new worship recording every two months—history had never seen anything like it. Christ For the Nations Institute (CFNI) in Dallas, Texas, also became recognized for their worship recordings. Launched from CFNI Dallas, Marty Nystrom's 1984 song, "As the Deer," became an international hit.

In 1986, I took my Bible school curriculum for training worship leaders, put it to longhand, and published my first book, *Exploring Worship: A Practical Guide to Praise and Worship*. It was the first book of its kind to blend both the devotional aspects of praise and worship with practical guidance for implementing worship in the local church. It was a forerunner book of sorts, and the Lord took it around the world. For example, the Russian translation went all over the Russian-speaking world because it was the first book on worship the churches in those regions had.

The worship movement continued to gain momentum in the late 1980s, but still, if you wanted to experience great worship, you probably had to go to a worship conference. It would take another decade for worship to go viral.

Questions for Wave Riders:

1. What are some books on worship that have impacted your life the most?

2. Did anyone in this group ever go to a worship conference? What one thing did you take away from the experience?

3. When did you first experience free worship that moved with rhythm and chord progressions? Do you have a story about it to tell us?

Chapter 5

WORSHIP IN THE 1990S

AMONG CHARISMATIC CHURCHES, the worship emphases of the 1980s continued to grow and spread. For example, churches developed worship teams, worship conferences proliferated, many churches practiced free worship supported by chord progressions and rhythm, musicians grew in their interest to lead worship, and songwriters increasingly honed their skill at writing new worship songs.

Then a new phenomenon surfaced: Churches began to hire *worship leaders* to serve in a full-time, paid staff capacity. If you had suggested in the 1960s that a church might hire someone to lead the singing, they would have laughed at you. But in the 1990s, pastors began to conduct job searches for an anointed worship leader who could join their staff. There never seemed to be enough capable worship leaders to fill the demand.

Something happened in 1992 that changed the worship movement in a powerful way. What was it?

The release of Ron Kenoly's worship album, *Lift Him Up* (Integrity Music). Compact discs (CDs) were just emerging, and this recording was available not only in cassette—you could also get it in CD! *Lift Him Up* went platinum, and not only put Integrity Music solidly on the map but put the worship movement on everyone's radar.

A decade earlier, if you had said to someone, "Let's put a microphone in the congregation, record the worship, and sell the recording," most Christians would have laughed at the idea. Who would want to buy a recording of a congregation singing four hymns on a Sunday morning? But by 1992, the world was ready, and sales of Ron Kenoly's album shattered every record. It sold like hotcakes through Christian bookstores and was carried around the world on the airwaves. Christian radio stations that usually played *Contemporary Christian Music* (CCM) began to get requests for *worship music*. Ultimately, worship music would rival and even overtake CCM in popularity.

Here's why the album *Lift Him Up* changed everything: America's Christian music industry awoke to the realization that the worship movement was more than a temporary fad. Instead of buying the latest CCM album, people were using their music dollars to buy worship albums. There was money to be made in worship music! Believers wanted worship music that was new, fresh, vibrant, intimate, creative, energetic, and

Spirit-empowered, and they were willing to pay for it. Nashville noticed.

The worship movement was becoming an industry.

Young people began to aspire to be worship leaders, and more and more colleges offered training to help prepare them. Amazingly, the number of musicians and singers being trained and released to minister in worship began to increase dramatically. There was a global need for anointed worship leaders, and God was raising up young people to pick up the baton.

The styles of worship didn't change much in the 1990s; what changed was the reach of worship music. By the latter part of the 1990s, worship music was *everywhere*—at the conferences, on the radio, on the TV, in the homes, in the cars, and in the churches.

If you wanted good worship in the 1980s, you had to attend a worship conference. But in the 90s, that changed. Conferences of all stripes began to feature worship leaders on their platforms. In fact, when conference organizers planned their guest lineup, landing a good worship leader became one of the first slots to fill. It no longer seemed to matter what kind of conference it was—whether a men's conference such as Promise Keepers, or a women's conference, or a youth conference, or a marriage conference, or a leadership conference—you were likely to experience strong worship.

The 1990s saw the release of many songs that are still favorites today. You may recognize some of these blockbusters:

- "I Could Sing of Your Love Forever" (Martin Smith, 1998)

- "I'm Coming Back to the Heart of Worship" (Matt Redman, 1998)

- "I Will Worship with All of My Heart" (David Ruis, 1993)

- "Our God Is an Awesome God" (Rich Mullins, 1996)

- "There Is None Like You" (Lenny LeBlanc, 1999)

- "Shout to the Lord" (Darlene Zschech, 1993)

- "Draw Me Close to You" (Kelly Carpenter, 1994)

Worship in the 1990s was passionate and spirited. With a contemporary sound, it was characterized by both vocal and physical freedom of movement. Love for Jesus was finding greater freedom of expression in more and more churches around the world. It was a great decade in the worship movement!

Now let's go to the new millennium.

Questions for Wave Riders:

1. What were some of the first worship recordings (albums) that really impacted and blessed you? What were some of the songs?

2. Talk about the statement, *The worship movement was becoming an industry.* What are your thoughts when you consider that statement?

3. If someone wants to become a worship leader today, what are some options for getting trained? What might be your recommendation to an aspiring worship leader?

Chapter 6

WORSHIP IN THE 2000S

AT THE TURN of the millennium, worship went mainstream. Let me explain what I mean. In the 90s, vibrant worship was to be found in select pockets of the Body of Christ—in certain churches or at certain events. But right around 2000, contemporary worship ignited across the Church worldwide. The Charismatics were no longer the only ones devoting themselves to contemporary, Spirit-filled worship; the Baptists joined the movement.

Several factors contributed to worship going mainstream, and I'll mention just a few. First of all, Christian radio was a huge catalyst. Christian radio began to broadcast the songs coming out of innovative ministries such as Vineyard and Hillsong. People wanted to worship in their cars and in their homes, so the Christian radio industry began to satisfy the demand. This awakened even more listeners in the Body of Christ to the worship movement.

Furthermore, stadium and outdoor events like Promise Keepers, Teen Mania, Creation, and Kingdom Bound featured powerful worship encounters. When young people (Gen Xers) experienced what God was doing in worship, they wanted in. Young people were leaving their Baptist churches in favor of Charismatic churches that were going with the new songs.

Baptist churches started to listen to their young people when they said things like, "We don't want hymns. We want contemporary worship." In response, many churches added a contemporary worship service on the weekend. Worshipers could choose between a *traditional* and *contemporary* service. The *traditional service* was typically a service with hymns in the 1960s tradition, often accompanied by a piano and/or organ; the *contemporary service* was typically a worship service with the latest songs from Christian radio, led by a worship band composed commonly of keyboards, guitars, bass guitar, drums, and singers.

Four things seemed to explode simultaneously.

Musicianship exploded. Droves of young people wanted to learn how to play guitar, keys, or drums. In the 1960s, it was rare to find a musician who could play for church worship; in the 2000s, musicians sprang up *everywhere*. One reason for this was that the new model of contemporary worship captivated young people, and they wanted to participate. Suddenly, it became desirable and popular for young people to learn to play a musical instrument for corporate worship. Some churches had so many aspiring musicians that they had to form multiple worship teams with different bands taking turns on Sundays. This explosion of musicianship is one of the most marvelous fruits of the worship movement.

Songwriting exploded. As churches began to sing the newest songs circulating in the Church, tremendous interest arose internationally to write new worship songs. For example, Hillsong Church's training school in Sydney, Australia, became known internationally as a great destination to develop your songwriting craft. New worship songs were being written and sung all around the world, and many musicians were producing recordings of their own original music. Songwriters like Chris Tomlin led the charge—his song "How Great Is our God" (2004) crashed on the shores of every continent.

Technology exploded. Somewhere around 2000, the entire sound engineering industry transitioned from analog to digital technology. The effects of the switch to digital were staggering. Much more could be done on a much smaller budget. The quality of sound reproduction increased significantly, and professional-grade equipment came within the reach of the general populace. In the 1980s, if you wanted to engineer a recording, you had to rent the facilities of an expensive recording studio; in the 2000s, musicians could set up a studio in their bedroom and replicate with their computer software the quality of a professional recording studio. The latest technologies suddenly became universally accessible.

And then, suddenly, there was the *release of hands*. Right around 2000, the Body of Christ found freedom to use their hands in worship. Until this time, only the Charismatics would lift their hands in worship, but in the 2000s, the Baptists joined in. For the Baptists to get on board with any expression of worship, it had to be *biblical*. They were like, "New songs? Well, the Bible talks about singing a new song to the Lord. So we're okay with your new songs."

"Lifting of hands? Well, we have quite a few verses in Scripture that refer to lifting our hands to the Lord. Since it's biblical, it's okay with us if you lift your hands in praise to God."

"Clapping hands in worship? Well, we have a verse for that one, too. So go ahead, clap your hands in praise to God!"

"A shout of praise? Well, that's in the Bible, too. We're told to shout to God with the voice of triumph. So if you want to shout to God in praise, we're okay with that as well."

It was right around 2000 that most churches and denominations opened to lifting hands, clapping hands, and shouts of joy in praise.

To say it another way, the Charismatics and Baptists joined together in the 2000s and became unified in their expressions of worship. The two streams that had run parallel for thirty years joined up again into one river of uniform expression.

Another factor contributed strongly to this trend: The Baptists became more tolerant or amicable toward the Charismatic practice of speaking in other tongues in worship to God. Many churches and groups who were formerly opposed to tongues seemed to lose their antagonism. It's not my purpose here to identify the *reasons* for this shift, but only to observe that it happened. Many churches took a stance along the lines of, "We don't teach or model tongues in our church, but if you pray in tongues in your private devotional life, we're okay with that, and you're welcome to become an active member in our church."

When the walls of antagonism toward tongues melted, tongue-talking Charismatics began to migrate to Baptist churches, bringing their instruments and worship styles with them.

For these and other reasons, the Baptists linked up with the worship movement in the 2000s. They changed—quite suddenly and dramatically—from a 1960s hymns model to a 2000s contemporary worship model. They said *yes* to new songs, to worship bands, and to expressive worship. In fact, the Baptists became so enthusiastic in devoting themselves to Davidic worship that it's almost as though some swapped places with the Charismatics. What I mean is some Baptist churches took on a more expressive, impassioned style while some Charismatic churches chose a more reserved, staid worship culture. In either case, the songs were contemporary.

Just as it was in the 1960s, worship today is once again uniform among Charismatics and Baptists. The gulf in worship styles that separated us in the 1970s has been bridged. It hardly matters the name on the church door; you're likely to experience similar worship on a Sunday morning in almost any church you enter these days.

This is also true for many historic and liturgical churches. For example, I was on a prayer walk not long ago in the Niagara Falls, New York, area and happened to stroll past a Lutheran Church (Missouri Synod) on a Saturday afternoon. I noticed some activity and thought I would poke my head in the front door and check things out. At the front of the sanctuary, a worship band was preparing for the Saturday evening contemporary service. They had keys, drums, guitar, bass, and singers. And they were singing the latest YouTube worship hits. I marveled as I witnessed their pre-service rehearsal because I was watching the fruit of the worship movement manifesting in a church typically known for preferring high liturgy. That scene was reflective of a worldwide phenomenon. Worship bands are leading the latest songs these days in

Charismatic, Pentecostal, Baptist, Lutheran, Episcopal, Church of Christ, and Roman Catholic churches.

The changes in worship over the past sixty years are nothing less than *spectacular*. YouTube is a powerful force today in globalizing worship.

This summarizes the picture of where we are today. The worship movement *took*. It was ordained of God, and it has been successful.

I celebrate where we are today. Musicians abound, new songs are springing up everywhere, worship is free and passionate, and the unity of the Church regarding worship is strong and beautiful. It's fantastic!

I love where we are—I just don't want to stay here. I want us to keep moving forward in God's purposes and plans for corporate worship. We're after God's heart for the upcoming decades so that we can catch the coming waves of Holy Spirit movement and partner with Him in the great harvest of souls that Scripture foretells.

Thank you for giving me time to tell the story of the past sixty years. When we understand our yesterday, we gain clearer perspective on where we are today. When we recognize today, we're able to prepare more effectively for tomorrow.

It's a new era. We all feel it and know it. We were hit by three storms in 2020: a political storm, a racial storm, and a pandemic storm (coronavirus). Interestingly, Jesus mentioned all three in one verse:

> *For nation will rise against nation, and kingdom*
> *against kingdom. And there will be famines,*
> *pestilences, and earthquakes in various places*
> (Matthew 24:7).

The original Greek word for *nation* is *ethnos*. Jesus was speaking of ethnicity against ethnicity, which describes the racial tensions we're currently feeling in the world.

When I read *kingdom against kingdom*, I see the political wars that America has known in recent times.

And *pestilences*, well, that's just another word for *pandemics* like COVID-19.

When Jesus pointed to these end-time storms, He indicated they would increase as His return draws near. Changes seem to be happening in our world with both increasing intensity and frequency.

In this kind of shifting world, we want to know where we're going. Specifically, we want to know where God will be taking us in worship so we can engage with our changing world and prepare the Bride of Christ for His return. As we look at the future of worship, therefore, we're looking at it through an end-time lens.

Come on, let's go there. Let's look at worship in a new era.

Questions for Wave Riders:

1. In what ways have you observed the Body of Christ gaining unity around worship?

2. Talk about using our hands in worship. Do you feel fully free to use your hands in offering your worship to God?

3. What are some ways we can continue to encourage young people to learn a musical instrument?

4. Have you ever been part of a songwriting retreat or a collaborative songwriting session?

5. How do you see worship shifting in the Church in the wake of the 2020 coronavirus pandemic?

Chapter 7

PLAYLIST WORSHIP

I CELEBRATE WHERE the Body of Christ is positioned in worship at the beginning of the 2020s. As already stated, we've got more musicians in the Church than ever. We have some of the most skillful songwriters of history and some of the best worship songs ever written. Today's worship is passionate, energetic, expressive, Christ-centered, and it's led by worship bands who have a Levitical calling to minister to the Lord. We're enjoying unparalleled levels of musical excellence. We're equipped with more worship-enhancing tools than any preceding generation. We have 24/7 worship and intercession in a manner church history has never seen. I celebrate all these improvements and enhancements with a grateful heart. God is *for* us, and He's taking us somewhere!

And yet, I've talked with some worship leaders who wonder if the global Church may be a bit *stuck* right now in our worship—as though we don't know how to move past where we are.

Well, where are we? When I take a sweeping, over-arching look at the global Church, I would describe our current place with the term *playlist worship*. What do I mean by that term? Let me explain.

YouTube Playlists

I have the idea of YouTube playlists in view. When you select a YouTube worship playlist on your device, the songs are stacked on each other, and they play sequentially. Sunday morning worship in many churches happens in a similar structure. It almost doesn't matter your nation, denomination, or church name, Sunday morning in many churches looks something like this.

The service is launched with a song. Once the first song is finished, the band then leads in a second song. Once the second song is finished, a third song is introduced. After the third song is done, a fourth song is sung. After the fourth song, the worship set is finished, and the service moves to the next thing in the service order (such as announcements or offering or prayer).

One. Two. Three. Four. Our churches do four songs on Sunday morning. We have excellent music, great lyrics, lots of passion, high energy, a cool atmosphere, and four songs.

We're back in the 1960s model of four songs. No matter the name on the door, almost all the churches are doing the same thing: four songs, one after the other. It's much like a YouTube playlist. In a playlist, you watch Track One, Track Two, Track Three, Track Four. On Sunday mornings, we do something very similar. It's almost as though we're replicating a YouTube playlist in our congregational meetings. That's why I'm describing the worship in many churches as *playlist worship*.

Once again, almost all the churches are singing the same songs—except they're not from a hardcover hymnal, but from the latest YouTube worship hits. Four in a row, one after the other. We're back in the 60s paradigm. How did we circle back here?

Playlist worship is a platform-driven kind of worship that can plow even if no one is in the room. Playlist worship can self-sustain even if everyone in the audience is watching online, or even if those in the room are disengaged.

You know it's playlist worship when the people in the room have the same experience as those watching the livestream.

You know it's playlist worship when you could have had the same experience by staying home and watching a YouTube playlist.

God never intended for corporate worship to be a playlist. There's something about congregational worship that is vital, living, breathing, and organic. Corporate worship is a dance, a divine romance. It's the song of the Bridegroom and the song of the Bride. It's a one-of-a-kind, never-seen-before, never-to-be-seen-again, dynamic love exchange.[1] It's a place of holy encounter with the living God.

The Worship Leader

We won't discover the breathing vitality of worship by following our digital click tracks, but by following the movements of *the* Worship Leader, the Holy Spirit. All the metaphors for His movements—wind, breath, oil, water—are *fluid*. There's nothing digital about the Holy Spirit's waves in worship.

If the Holy Spirit truly is the Worship Leader in your church, then honor Him. Don't limit Him to a set list. Don't tether the Breath to a playlist. Playlists click, but true worship breathes. True worship is a wending, reciprocating conversation of loyalty and devotion with our Beloved.

The worshipers of the world have a message for the worship leaders of the world: We didn't come to the house for your set list. We came for the "you had to be there" moments in the room. We came for a living, organic, spontaneous, raw, visceral, symphonic, romantic dance. We came to participate in the weaving of a holy tapestry of worship such as history has not yet seen, nor ever again will see. We want worship where there's nuance, ebb, flow, passion, tears, and joy. We want worship in Spirit and truth.

Please don't suppose that, with my term *playlist worship*, I'm critical of where we are. I'm simply pointing out that we've paused at this overlook, and I'm persuaded God is going to keep moving us forward on this highway of holiness. He's going to help us continue to develop and mature so we can flow with the Spirit's progressive movements.

Online Versus In-Person

In March 2020, the coronavirus outbreak caused many churches around the world to close their doors temporarily as our globe fought to contain the spread. During that time, many churches conducted online services, and as a consequence, many believers became comfortable with doing church online at home. When churches were finally able to gather again, many had a fraction of the attendance they had before coronavirus. This triggered an ecclesiological crisis, and many churches asked, "What do we need to do to get believers to return to our corporate gatherings?"

We could strengthen our preaching—but that wouldn't actually bring them back because they could still enjoy the impact of our sermons by watching the webcast in their pajamas at home.

We could strengthen the excellence of our worship ministry—but playlist worship doesn't bring them back to the congregation because the impact of playlist worship is the same whether you're in the church building or watching the webcast at home.

What will bring them back to church?

Some will return to our church gatherings regardless of what we do because they're committed disciples of Christ and they're fiercely resolved to obey all of Scripture, including Hebrews 10:25, *"Not forsaking the assembling of ourselves together, as is the manner of some, but exhorting one another, and so much the more as you see the Day approaching."*

But what about the believers who don't yet have a conviction about obeying that Scripture? Until they gain that conviction, what can we do to win them back to corporate worship? We'll need to offer them more than playlist worship. We'll need to offer something in the gathering that can't be received by staying home.

For those who have zeal for God's house, I've got some great news (see John 2:17)! The most vital, life-giving elements of worship are dynamics that can be experienced only by being present in the room. Online worship is great when it's your only option, but it can never replace the glory of God's house.

There are some elements of worship that can't be accessed in an online format, and these will become increasingly precious in the lives of Jesus' disciples. What are some of those elements? Let me list a few of them because you'll want to watch for these gifts of grace to find greater prominence in the next wave of worship:

- the Lord's Table
- laying on of hands prayer ministry
- anointing with oil
- corporate intercession
- water baptisms
- altar calls
- praying for one another
- fellowship and mutual encouragement

These aspects of worship are experienced not online but when we gather. Powerful things happen when God's people gather together to worship! Jesus promised to be present among believers when they *gather* (see Matt. 18:20).

Be Present for His Presence

Corporate worship is meant to be experienced and expressed in the moment. It's such a vigorous and vibrant engagement with Jesus that you really have to be in the room to experience the fullness of the encounter.

The Presence of Jesus is a present reality. To experience Presence, you must be present. Thomas learned this when Jesus presented Himself to His disciples after

His resurrection, but Thomas wasn't there (see John 20:24). He missed it. Maybe he determined in his heart to be present next time Jesus showed up because, when Jesus presented Himself to His disciples a second time, Thomas was in the room. This time he was able to touch Jesus personally (see John 20:26–27).

There's something so *present* about corporate worship that, when Jesus manifests His Presence among His people, we end up saying to those who weren't there, "You missed it! This was not the time to stay home and watch the webcast. You should have been there. God was in the house!"

Be present in His presence.

A wave of worship is coming where you're going to want to be present in the room to experience it.

Worshipers find themselves dissatisfied with Zoom Church. Why? No miracles are performed on the sick, no demons are cast out, and there's no personal prayer ministry, no water baptisms, and no song of the people.

I'm grateful when online services can augment what we offer and lengthen our reach, but they can't replace the congregation. The Father just wants all the family to come over, gather round, and join Him at the table. We know this because that's the kind of worship we see in the book of Revelation. Congregational worship is here to stay, forever.

His Presence Is the Draw

The international COVID-19 lockdown of churches in 2020 only served to highlight something that has always been true: There's something irreplaceable about the role of corporate worship in the life of a local church and of every believer.

In the coming wave of worship, God will be doing things in our midst that will be experienced only by those who are present. Playlist worship? You can stay home and enjoy that on the livestream. But we'll be touching realms of worship so present and vital that people will get in their cars so they can come and experience it.

Presence worship is the wave of the future.

Questions for Wave Riders:

1. A lot of people are grappling with the tension between online worship and in-person worship. Where do you see God taking us? In what ways do you agree or disagree with the author in this chapter?

2. Have you felt like the Church is a little stuck right now in worship? In what way?

3. Do you like the term *Presence worship*? What does it mean to you?

4. What can we do to give greater prominence to the interactive elements of worship listed in this chapter, such as Communion, anointing with oil, etc.?

Note

1. I explore this more in my book *Following the River: A Vision for Corporate Worship.*

Chapter 8

READ THE OCEAN

WORSHIP LEADERS ARE surfers. We're always trying to find a wave of Holy Spirit momentum in worship, and once we're riding it, we want to take it all the way to the shore. As a worship leader, I've always connected implicitly with the imagery of ocean surfing, and yet my understanding of the connection has been limited because I've never actually surfed.

My understanding of surfing grew during one of my trips to Southern California. I flew into Orange County in preparation for a weekend of ministry, and my host and friend, Steve Skolos, treated me to lunch at the Dana Point Ritz-Carlton Hotel. Steve's friend, Mike Fanning, also joined us for lunch. When dining at the swanky Ritz, you really can't afford to do dinner, but the lunch prices are manageable.

The quaint and charming city of Dana Point is a balmy destination on California's coast. A high bluff overlooks the surf, and sitting atop the cliff is the upscale Ritz-Carlton. One wall of the hotel's posh restaurant is nothing but glass. We sat by the glass wall and nibbled our sandwiches while relishing the panoramic view of the bay. Below us, surfers had gathered at a certain favored patch of beach and were hunting for rideable waves.

In the course of conversation with my friends, it came out that both Steve and Mike are surfers. As soon as I realized I was seated with surfers, I decided to maximize the moment. I wanted a better understanding of the dynamics of the sport, so I took advantage of the opportunity and tried to draw them out. I said, "Tell me about the art of surfing. What's going on?"

Paddling for the Sweet Spot

Steve and Mike told me surfers are always trying to get to where the big waves are. The best waves are formed by the confluence of strong winds and a properly contoured ocean floor. Some beaches hold a special draw for surfers because of their renown for producing the biggest waves.

Waves come in groups—which was new information for me—and they said that the largest wave in a group is the middle one. The number of waves in a group will vary, so surfers will try to figure out how many waves are present in any given group. Every wave is carefully examined so that, when the largest wave in the group begins to form, it can be identified. For example, if there are thirteen waves in a certain group, the largest wave is likely to be the seventh. Surfers will let good waves go by because they're holding out for the best one.

Once surfers sense a large wave beginning to form, they'll try to position themselves to catch it by swimming vigorously toward the sweet spot. I said, "Excuse me. *Sweet spot?* Waves have sweet spots?"

Steve and Mike said, "Yes. When the right wave comes along, there's a sweet spot on the wave that you want to mount. If you're a few feet to the left or to the right of the sweet spot, you may as well just let that wave go past because you're not positioned properly to capture it."

When they said this, certain experiences in my spiritual journey instantly made sense to me. Let me explain.

I'm a revivalist, a Glory junkie. When it comes to the movements of the Holy Spirit in worship, I can't ever get enough. I always want more fire, more Presence, more oil, more water, more Word, more understanding, more tears, more laughter, more visions, more angelic encounters, more glory clouds, more repentance, more water baptisms, more speaking in other tongues, more prophesying, more apostolic preaching, more terror of the Lord, more dancing, more prostrating in holiness, more healings, more authority over demonic powers, more lightnings of God, more signs and wonders, more love-sickness, more Kingdom keys, more open doors in the Spirit. I always want *more!*

In my eager pursuit for more of Jesus, I've made pilgrimage several times to revival hotspots. Why would I do that? Because I've taken my cues from John the Baptist. I reckon the only way the people of Israel could have experienced the revival under the ministry of John the Baptist was by making pilgrimage to the wilderness to actually attend the baptism services. That's why I'm willing to make pilgrimage when I hear of a powerful move of the Spirit in another city. If God's moving, I want in!

I can think of five U.S. cities, off the top of my head, where I've made pilgrimage over the years because I had heard that God was moving in a powerful way through a certain ministry in that city. Each time, I came away feeling like I had missed the wave. I watched again and again while people next to me would catch the Spirit's wave, get swept up in the love of Christ, bask in the fiery flow of the Holy Spirit's movements, and I would remain unmoved. I wanted to catch the wave but seemingly couldn't. I would wonder, *What's wrong with me? Why is my neighbor able to catch this wave, and I'm not?* In fact, some conferences were even titled, *Catch the Wave*. I was hungry enough, desperate enough, eager enough, but I simply didn't experience the same power as my neighbor. I wondered, *Is there something about my life that's displeasing to the Lord?*

But now I realize I wasn't positioned at the time to catch that wave. Because of my personal spiritual season at the time, it wasn't my time for that wave. My neighbor was positioned for the wave, but I wasn't. The wave was good, strong, energized by the Holy Spirit, and designed by God to refresh and ignite the Body of Christ, but it wasn't my wave. God would have another wave for me at a later time, and I would need to wait for it with expectant endurance. But for now, I would watch this huge wave roll right past me. I longed to surf it with all my heart, but it wasn't the right time.

Steve and Mike's explanation of sweet spots in waves helped me interpret the disappointment I've experienced as I've watched multiple waves move right past me. And their explanation also infused me with hope because there are more waves yet to come in the ocean of God's love. I have much expectation in my heart that God is going to send a great wave for which I *will* be positioned.

Surfers, therefore, are looking for two things. They're looking for the right wave, and then they're looking for the right placement on that wave. When there are others in the water, it's a bit of a race to see who can paddle to the sweet spot first. First one to mount the sweet spot gets to take that wave for a ride!

Get in the Water

While enjoying our lunch, my friends made two statements about surfing that struck me with such strength that I wrote them down. They said, "You don't learn any-thing about surfing until you get in the water." You can watch lots of YouTube tutorials, buy the best equipment, paint your surfboard, and hang out with surfers on the beach, but you'll never learn how to surf until you actually get in the water.

You learn to surf by doing it wrong a thousand times. The more times you fail, the more you learn and the better you become. This also reminds me of worship. Sometimes the best way to learn how to lead worship is just to jump into the waters and do it wrong a thousand times.

Like snowflakes, no two waves are alike. Every engagement with the next wave will be different from anything ever before experienced. This is why riding the waves of worship is filled with so much "trial and error." When training apprentices to lead worship, therefore, let's provide an experimental environment where it's safe to tumble. The more we blow it and then learn from our mistakes, the more skillful we'll become.

Then my friends said this about surfing: "It's when you're out in the water that you learn to read the ocean."

I said, "Excuse me. *Read the ocean?*"

They said, "Yes. Surfers learn to read the ocean. They study its movements, and with enough experience, they can learn how to anticipate what the ocean is about to do."

Waves come with a powerful undertow. If surfers don't read the waves wisely, the ocean can hurt them. They must learn to go after the right thing while also avoiding the wrong thing.

Steve and Mike told me, "When you learn to read the ocean, you can identify when the big wave is beginning to form, and you can determine whether the sweet spot is reachable."

Let me apply that spiritually. Those who exercise themselves at reading the ocean of the Holy Spirit's movements can develop an ability to identify when a great wave of Holy Spirit momentum is beginning to form and can determine if they're positioned to capture the next wave.

What can worshipers learn from these elementary principles of surfing? Get in the water. Learn to read the ocean of God's movements in the earth.

When surfers mount a wave and ride it, they're doing three things. With their eyes they're watching, with their feet they're feeling, and with their hands they're balancing. This is what worship leaders do.

As we read the ocean of God's movements today, what kind of waves can we expect to come in the days ahead? Let me say it clearly and honestly: I don't have divine information on where God will be taking us in worship in the coming decades. I want to be careful to stay in my sphere and not claim insight that is greater than my portion.

With that disclaimer, I'm willing to share with you some of the things that I *believe* and *hope* will be coming.

Questions for Wave Riders:

1. When you consider surfing as a metaphor for worship leading, what insights do you see? Is it a helpful metaphor? Can you think of a biblical metaphor that comes close to it?

2. Have you ever made a trip to a certain city because you heard God was doing something significant there? Tell us your story.

3. In what way have you ever just jumped in the water with the Holy Spirit?

4. What have you learned about reading the ocean of the Holy Spirit's movements in worship?

Chapter 9

PHILISTINE CARTS

JESUS TOLD US the Father is seeking worshipers who will worship Him in Spirit and in truth (see John 4:23). By reducing His descriptors of worship to two words (Spirit and truth), Jesus seemed to indicate the stuff that makes up worship is plain and simple.

Corporate worship has always had a human tendency toward the complicated. In recent decades, it has attracted a variety of accoutrements. In our humanity, we have a carnal proclivity to add human means to the implementation of the Great Commission (see Matt. 28:18–20). I use the term *human means* in the same way David Brainerd did—the famous missionary to Native Americans. He discovered his ministry was most impactful when he had literally no human resources to enable his ministry and was utterly dependent upon the Holy Spirit to move supernaturally through his preaching. This dependence drove him to intercede intensely for the Gospel to win his hearers.

Regarding human means, one thing Brainerd lacked was a believing translator to help him minister to the natives. His only translator was a drunken native unbeliever who intoned the translation with no conviction, and yet Brainerd watched in wonder as the Holy Spirit struck the hearts of his listeners like a hammer with the gift of repentance. As he recounted his evangelistic triumphs through the power of the Spirit, he marveled over and over how God captured hardened hearts "without means"—that is, without any human strengths or resources to account for the impact. God used plain and not elaborate means.

In contrast, when it comes to worship today, we have an abundance of human means. We have the most worship tools history has ever witnessed. We have cool décor, perfect temperatures, comfortable seating, magnificent lighting, sound loops, pads, multitracks, click tracks, digital boards, talkback microphones, autotune software, in-ear monitors, subwoofers, high definition jumbotron screens, strobe lights, sound compression, reverb, smoke machines, and more. We have so many aids and implements that it almost seems possible to pull off worship services without the Holy Spirit's help. Equipment itself is not the difficulty; the problem is our human tendency to lean on natural means to achieve a spiritual end.

What should we do in an age of pervasive props? We must return, over and over, to the simplicity of worship—to worship in Spirit and truth. We must return continually to the *heart* of worship.[1]

Moving the Ark

When I consider our human tendency to depend on human means to implement corporate worship, I'm reminded of the story in the Old Testament when David escorted the ark of the covenant to Zion. Called "the Presence," the ark was the place where God established His Presence in Israel, making it the primary physical representation of Israel's worship (see Heb. 6:19). David wanted God's Presence at home in Zion, which meant the ark needed to be moved from its temporary storage in Abinadab's home. Therefore, he placed the ark on a wooden cart and began the trek for Jerusalem. Here's the biblical account:

> *So they set the ark of God on a new cart, and brought it out of the house of Abinadab, which was on the hill; and Uzzah and Ahio, the sons of Abinadab, drove the new cart. And they brought it out of the house of Abinadab, which was on the hill, accompanying the ark of God; and Ahio went before the ark. Then David and all the house of Israel played music before the Lord on all kinds of instruments of fir wood, on harps, on stringed instruments, on tambourines, on sistrums, and on cymbals. And when they came to Nachon's*

*threshing floor, Uzzah put out his hand to the ark
of God and took hold of it, for the oxen stumbled.
Then the anger of the Lord was aroused against
Uzzah, and God struck him there for his error; and
he died there by the ark of God* (2 Samuel 6:3–7).

We're told twice in the story that Abinadab's house
was on a hill because we're intended to visualize a cart
rolling down a hill. As the cart was drawn downhill by
the oxen, it gained momentum and accelerated. When
the oxen came to some uneven terrain, they stumbled,
and the ark almost tipped over. Uzzah grabbed the ark to
save it from capsizing, and God struck him dead on the
spot for his error.

What was Uzzah's error? He violated God's instructions in Numbers 4:11–15. God told Moses that, when the
tabernacle's furniture was being moved, the ark must be
covered and carried by poles on the shoulders of Levites.
Furthermore, God specifically said, *"They shall not touch
any holy thing, lest they die"* (Num. 4:15). If they would
carry the ark by poles on their shoulders, the Levites
would never have necessity to touch the ark. But Uzzah
touched the holy ark, and that's why he died.

Since God had commanded the Levites to move the
ark on their shoulders, this leaves us wondering, *Why,
then, did David move the ark with a cart and two oxen?*
The answer seems to be, *Because the Philistines moved the
ark with a cart.*

Let me remind you about that part of the story.

In a tragic turn of events, the ark of the covenant had been captured in battle by the Philistines (see 1 Sam. 4). While the ark was in their territory, the Philistines were plagued with pestilence, sickness, and death. Desperate to escape God's judgments, they placed the ark on a wooden cart, hitched two milk cows to it, and watched to see if the cows would carry the ark to Israel. Sure enough, the cows headed directly toward the Israelite town of Beth Shemesh (see 1 Sam. 6:1–18). God Himself caused those cows—who would have never left their milking calves on their own—to return the ark to Israel. Clearly, God honored the Philistines' idea of using a cart.

Years later, when David decided to move the ark to Zion, instead of consulting Scripture for the proper order, he placed the ark on a cart. The Philistines' precedent seemed to be a compelling method. David may have been thinking something like, *When the Philistines put the ark on a cart, God blessed their efforts and guided the cows right back to Israel. Since God blessed their cart on that occasion, that must be a good method to move the ark.* Whatever his reasons, David chose to move God's Presence with Philistine methods. As a consequence, Uzzah was killed, and the ark was detained at another temporary residence.

David would learn a tough lesson from this botched attempt: *Consult God first.* When he moved the ark the second time, he consulted the divine order and appointed

Levites to carry the ark on their shoulders. Thus, his second attempt to bring the ark to Zion was favored of the Lord (see 2 Sam 6:12–15).

Worship Carts

Like David, we also take our cues sometimes from the Philistines—that is, from the world. Maybe we're wowed by the way worldly bands will move large auditoriums of people with their music, or maybe we're grabbed by their sound. Hitting copy-paste, we'll repeat some of the same means in congregational worship. Search for the right YouTube tutorial, and you can probably take an online class from the Philistines on cart mobilization.

What does the Philistine cart represent? Human mechanisms to move God's Presence in corporate worship.

The people of Israel seemed to love the cart, David seemed pleased enough with the cart, and the Levites loved the cart. Only one Person was unhappy with the cart—the one for whom the whole thing was meant. The ride was smooth to David, but rough to God.

If you'll allow me a little sarcasm, it seems that contemporary worship has some real cool carts. We've become expert cart builders. We're skillful at crafting models of worship powerful enough to accomplish our ministry goals. Our worship carts have shock absorbers, padding, wide wheels, and fancy hubcaps. Do some surfing on the web, and you'll be able to study worship carts from all over the world. There's the England cart, the Australia cart, the Brazil cart, the Africa cart, the California cart, the North Carolina cart, the Kansas City cart, the Dallas cart, the Atlanta cart. You can search until you find the model that's right for you. Yes, I'm being a little sarcastic, but I'm doing it with a smile—because I realize we're all doing our best to develop a model of worship that is powerful and reproduceable.

We might do well to ask ourselves the question, In what ways do we take cues from the Philistines to move the Presence? In what ways do we tend toward the mechanical in worship?

For starters, it's helpful to acknowledge that this is an unremitting, universal temptation from which none of us are exempt. We're always inclined to favor the fast and easy. The first step in overcoming is to realize we must be on constant alert for the mechanical in worship.

When the energy of corporate worship derives more from the mechanics on the platform than the Spirit's activity in the midst of the congregation, we may want to ask ourselves if we've gotten into a mechanical cart mode.

Levites Love Carts

Levites love carts. Why? Because steering a cart is way easier than carrying something on your shoulders. When you put that bar across your shoulder, feel the weight of the Presence, and then head for Zion, carrying that thing is not so easy. The bar digs into your neck and chafes your shoulder. You feel the weight in your back and legs, your muscles tighten, and you break a sweat. Carrying the Presence is hard work.

Carts, in comparison, are way easier. For starters, carts are more labor efficient. A cart requires only two Levites, but carrying it on poles requires four. And those four will tire quickly, needing to be relieved by four others. You may even need multiple teams. "Two Levites and a cart"—it's the easiest way to move.

Furthermore, you can get a lot more momentum a lot faster with a cart. Carts are faster and more efficient at producing crowd energy and enthusiasm.

Besides, carts are less expensive. They take a smaller chunk of a church's budget. In contrast, when the Levites carried the ark on their shoulders to Zion, David sacrificed animals every six paces. That meant the entire processional demanded a much larger budget.

Carts go further faster. When Levites carry the ark on their shoulders, the pace is painfully slow. The slower they walk, the longer the worship service.

One of the greatest benefits of good worship carts is that they make for shorter worship services and shorter meetings. You can take a 30-minute worship service, tighten it up, and get it down to 20 minutes. Once you have corporate worship down to 20 minutes, with a little bit of work you can deliver the same punch in 17 minutes. And once you've trimmed it to 17 minutes, it's really not that difficult to make it a strong 15-minute worship encounter. This makes for smooth, streamlined services that attract larger crowds.

Sarcasm aside now, I see a wave of worship coming in which the prevailing question will not be, "What's the least amount of time we can devote to corporate worship and still have a vibrant service?" Rather, the question will be more like, "Now that Jesus is with us, how can we host Him well?"

God's not downsizing worship, nor does He view it as a tool for church growth. It's not a vehicle to accomplish a certain end, but is an end in itself. Love is its own end.

To walk with Jesus means we must slow to His pace.

I see a wave of worship coming in which the prevailing question will not be, "What's the least amount of money we can allocate to corporate worship and still have a vibrant worship department?" When King David was figuring out his national budget for worship, he assigned substantial resources for the support of psalmists 24/7 in the Lord's house. It takes money to finance nonstop worship. God's heart for worship is not so much for a fiery 15-minute Sunday morning encounter, but more for a 24/7 burning reality where the fire on the altar of our hearts never goes out (see Lev. 6:12).

Walk It Out

When the Levites shouldered the ark and walked it to Zion, they broke a sweat. This helps us appreciate that the Levitical ministry of worship is *supposed* to be hard work.

Leading worship is rigorous, and God wants His Levites feeling the rigor of it. He wants us doing the hard work of carrying the worship service on our shoulders. He wants us to feel the ground with every step, and to move forward slowly and carefully as we make pilgrimage together into the heart of God. As my friend Dan Bohi told me, he tries to slow down so he can catch up with Jesus.

When it comes to walking and moving with the Holy Spirit, stay low and go slow.

When worship leaders are carrying the ark of His Presence, they're doing three things. With their eyes they're watching, with their feet they're feeling, and with their hands they're balancing.

When you're feeling the ground with your feet, you might occasionally look at the next song on your set list and realize that, if you go with that song, you'll end up detoured. To keep going straight ahead into the heart of God sometimes means doing something outside our preparation. Keeping your balance over terrain you weren't prepared for is weighty, sobering, and rigorous.

Living Movers

May I tell you something about God? He likes to be moved, not by mechanical things, but by living creatures. When the Son of God was transported in the Old Testament, His chariot was composed of four living creatures (in 1 Chron. 28:18, Jesus' car was called *the chariot*). Ezekiel went into quite a lengthy description of this vehicle when he saw it (see Ezek. 1, 3, and 10). One of the most compelling elements in Ezekiel's descriptions is that every aspect of this chariot is *alive*. The four cherubim are spirits, the wheels are spirits, the rims of the wheels are spirits—the whole thing is a confederation of living spirits that work together to transport the Glory (Jesus).

It seems consistent, then, that God would want the Presence transported by Levites and not by a cart. Shoulders represent responsibility, and God wants His Levites to feel the weight of their responsibility as shepherds. He wants us to carry a love burden for the flock. We're sobered by the fact that there are people in the room who will or will not connect with God based on how we shoulder the moment.

Corporate worship isn't a set list but a *journey*, and worship ministries are *shepherds*. We're taking God's people somewhere. We're on a Psalm 84 pilgrimage, and we're making our way together to Zion. We're not called to pull off successful worship sets; we're called to lead people to Jesus. We're on a quest to appear before

God. Every worship service is like a Psalm 84 pilgrimage. There's a sense of *launch*, of *journey*, and ultimately of *destination*.

When we meet up with Jesus, we're at our destination and have no place else to go.

When God's people come together for a meeting, it appears on the surface that we're gathered, but we're not. At the start of the meeting, we're still scattered—mentally and emotionally. As the service begins, worship ministries seek to gather the flock and gain a sense of corporate identity. Then we can move together in our journey to connect with God. We want worship services where we actually go somewhere. We want to arrive somewhere in the Spirit where there's a sense of completion and finish. Our hearts will never be fully satisfied until *"each one appears before God in Zion"* (Ps. 84:7). We want God!

Presence/Production Tension

My friend Caleb Culver told me the next wave of worship will focus more on Presence and less on perfection. God will inspire things that are counterintuitive to some of today's trends. Some of today's trends feature dark sanctuaries, cool lighting, arc lamps, and smoke machines. We're not opposed to these things, but we're not fooled by them, either. Production is not Presence. It's great when technology can be a helpful, creative tool, but it can never slake our thirst for having Jesus' Presence with us.

Mechanical means of production tend toward a concert culture in worship. Concert culture worship has become an international industry. As Jeremy Riddle has said, this is the best time in worship history to be a worship leader for all the wrong reasons. As we move forward in worship in the coming decades, God is going to help us remove a celebrity culture in which worship leaders and songwriters are placed on a pedestal of fame. When my friend Laura Souguellis spoke with me about Riddle's statement and celebrity culture, she said that worship leaders are sometimes turned into celebrities. When that happens, they fight the temptation to protect their public image. They can lose the freedom to be a snot-soaked mess on the floor, and instead find themselves fighting to maintain a reputable appearance.

As we search for the next wave of worship, we're going to give our worship ministries the freedom to explore, collapse, twirl, prostrate, make mistakes, and look bad. When surfers are trying to catch a wave, they're always blowing it publicly. We're going to keep letting go of the celebrity culture and allow our worship leaders to miss the wave in public.

When Electric Carts Lose Power

One way God helps us recognize our mechanical tendencies in worship is by snarling our electronics. I've heard stories from worship leaders about the electric power going out during a worship service. In the scramble to compensate, they said they've observed and learned some things.

For example, my friend Clayton Brooks told me of the time the power went out in their building just hours before a special night of worship at their church. The night had been promoted for weeks, and everyone was excited about coming together and worshiping without being distracted by time constraints. When the electricity went out that afternoon, Clayton was really discouraged and almost canceled the event. But then he decided to try an alternative. They wheeled a grand piano into the atrium, set up a hundred chairs around it, and had an acoustic evening of worship. Clayton said it was really challenging to lead, but there was something unique and special about the interactive elements of seeing and hearing each other worship. There was a contagion of faith in the room. Clayton said it turned out to be everyone's favorite night that they talked about for months afterward.

I'll mention three other stories briefly to help further illustrate this point.

Daisy Burgan wrote to me about being in a meeting when the power went out in the heat of summer. Instinctively, everyone just kept singing. The drummer exited the cage and got on the djembe. Daisy wrote, "You could hear the congregation, and we all sounded like one voice. It was beautiful, and Holy Spirit was on it."

Tracy Whitehead wrote me about a worship set at the International House of Prayer in Kansas City that was led by Cory Asbury. A thunderstorm hit, and the power went out just as Cory was singing, "I am my Beloved's and He is mine, so come into Your garden and take delight in me." Tracy said that Cory came forward to the edge of the stage, sat down with his guitar, and just kept singing the song. Tracy wrote, "It was so incredible and beautifully overwhelming to hear everyone's voices all around me in the dark!"

Tammy Oliver wrote me about a time her husband, the pastor, was finishing the sermon and he asked the worship team to come. When they reached the platform, he just happened to say, "I'm really not trying to be dramatic"—*bam!*—the power went out. The acoustic player grabbed his guitar, and the congregation turned on their phone lights. Tammy wrote, "It was a beautiful moment as we sang and worshiped, and several came to the altar for salvation!"

Again, moments of production failure sometimes serve to help us keep our eyes on that which is truly important—the face of Jesus.

Altar of Earth

The Philistine cart motif of this chapter has a twin metaphor in the book of Exodus. God gave specific instructions to Moses regarding the kind of altar He wanted built for worship:

> *An altar of earth you shall make for Me, and you shall sacrifice on it your burnt offerings and your peace offerings, your sheep and your oxen. . . . And if you make Me an altar of stone, you shall not build it of hewn stone; for if you use your tool on it, you have profaned it* (Exodus 20:24–25).

My friend Dick Grout pointed out to me the *plainness* of this altar. It was to be made of earth, and if made with stone, the stones must not be hewn or carved.

Worship isn't chiseled, it's earthy.

Heaven's Worship

Where God is taking us in worship is displayed in its greatest biblical clarity in the book of Revelation. We want worship on the earth as it is in heaven. When you examine heaven's worship, at least as John experienced it, you'll notice this intriguing feature: There's only one musical instrument used in worship—harps. (Trumpets are also mentioned in Revelation, but they're used for heralding, not worship.)

What should we conclude from this observation? I'm not sure, but the book of Revelation gives me the impression that the worship of heaven is primarily vocally driven, not instrument driven. (I've not been there, smile, so I'm not being dogmatic.) Harps seem to be used, not as a means to drive corporate worship, but as a means to give expression to the musician's wholehearted affections for the Lamb.

I'm also intrigued by the things John *didn't* mention about heaven's worship. He never saw a platform, or a sound system, or a worship leader.

What grips us about heaven's worship? Its simplicity and organic vitality.

The worship of heaven is organic, not mechanical. The simplicity of *"worship in Spirit and truth"* seems to capture its essence. This is the wave of the future.

Questions for Wave Riders:

1. Have you ever witnessed the Holy Spirit do a remarkable work "without human means"? Share it with the group.

2. In what ways are we tempted to move God's Presence with mechanical methods?

3. *Leading worship is rigorous.* In what way might you agree or disagree?

4. Talk about the statement, *Worship isn't chiseled, it's earthy.* What does that mean to you?

Note

1. Matt Redman's story behind the writing of his song, "Heart of Worship," is a marvelous example of this. You can find the story easily online at pages such as https://www.eden.co.uk/blog/worship/heart-of -worship-the-story-behind-the-song-p11688/.

Chapter 10

THE SONG OF THE PEOPLE

SONGS ARE MUSICAL prayers, and we use our songs to help people pray and connect with God. Singing is a marvelous gift in the Spirit to help us encounter God. One of the primary objectives of corporate worship, therefore, is to release the song of the people.

Releasing the song of the people is a formidable goal, however, because the natural inclination of weak human hearts in the Presence of a holy God is to hide our faces and suppress our voices. The Lord is always saying to His beloved Bride, *"Let me see your face, let me hear your voice; for your voice is sweet, and your face is lovely"* (Song 2:14). He's always coaxing us to open up because our universal tendency is to shut down.

In keeping with this human trend, the tendency of corporate worship throughout church history has been for congregations to grow increasingly quiet and passive, and for platform ministries to become increasingly directive and dominant. Reversing this chronic trend is a daunting task.

Drawing out the voice of the Bride requires intentional leadership. In the coming wave, I see the worship ministries of the world devoting themselves to this goal. The skill of worship ministries will be measured, not so much by their ability to sing their songs with excellence, but by their ability to unlock and release the song of the people.

How Did We Lose the Song of the People?

As observed earlier, the global Body of Christ finds itself back in a 1960s model of worship—singing four songs in succession. When the songs are done, the worship is done. Most worshipers don't exercise themselves to sing past the song, so we don't experience the song of the people.

But it wasn't always like this. In the Charismatic movement of the 1970s, for example, the song of the people burst forth with great fervor and dynamism. It carried into the 80s, and even held up somewhat in the 90s. But we've lost that vitality and grown quiet again.

Today, we're singing the songs of the songwriters, we're singing the songs of the platforms, and we're singing the songs of the worship bands; but we've lost the song of the people.

We enter our church facilities on Sunday mornings, grab our coffee of choice in the lobby, bring our mugs into the sanctuary, and sip on our lattes while the worship band releases the passionate praises of Jesus. We stand and sip, watch the worship band light up, follow the lyrics on the screens, and warm our hands to the bonfire on the platform.

The worship warms us, and we applaud it approvingly, but it doesn't draw out our song.

Why have we lost the song of the people? I'd like to submit one reason for your consideration: We haven't carried with us the worship gifts God gave us in the 1970s, 80s, and 90s. Let me explain those gifts.

As mentioned in chapter three, in the 1970s the Lord gave the Church a gift in what was called *singing in the Spirit* or *free worship*. It was vocally driven, energized by the congregation not the platform, and was supported by a sustained I chord (often with an instrument, but sometimes without). People would sing their own song to the Lord with freedom of vocal range and vocabulary. Everyone would sing simultaneously as they felt inspired by the Holy Spirit, and the songs would meld together into a chorale of unified praise. Worshipers would weave seamlessly between English and other tongues. When a known song was sung and then finished, the worship would still continue because the entire congregation would continue in its own spontaneous songs of love and joy. The saints sang their hearts out to the Lord!

This form of spontaneous singing in the Spirit was a sweet gift from above, but some churches resisted it at the time because it was usually associated with singing in other tongues. When some of those churches joined the worship movement in the 2000s, this practice of singing in the Spirit wasn't part of their worship history, so it didn't even occur to them to pick it up. They picked up new songs, lifting hands, clapping hands, and even shouting, but not singing in the Spirit. As a result, it fell away from the practices of most groups in the Body of Christ—even from those who had formerly practiced it. It was the song of the people, and it was lost.

Then, in the 1980s, the Lord gave us another gift—He showed us how to add rhythms and chord progressions to free worship (see chapter four). The changing chords made for greater variety of song, and the addition of rhythm made for varying degrees of intensity and passion. This practice of singing freely in the Spirit to the accompaniment of rhythm and chord progressions was a sweet gift from heaven, and it really empowered and released the song of the people. But again, the churches that didn't receive 70s singing in the Spirit didn't receive the 80s practice of doing it with rhythm and chord progressions, either. By the time those churches relaxed their resistance to tongues in the 2000s, they didn't even know there was a gift from the 1980s to be accessed. This gift had empowered the song of the people, but in the 2000s it fell off the radar of most groups in the global Church.

The worship models that arose in the 2000s did not practice, for the most part, spontaneous singing in the Spirit. When young worship leaders joined the worship movement, they were shown how to lead in hymns but not in spiritual songs (see Eph. 5:19). Consequently, the song of the people has grown quiet, and we're back in a 1960s worship paradigm.

Said another way, we leapt thirty years from the 1960s to the 2000s and didn't pause to pick up the gifts God had granted in the intervening years. Understanding what we've lost, the call of my message is simply this: Let's recover those gifts! Let's revisit those altars of worship, pick back up those gracious gifts, and include them in our legacy as we explore the potential of worship in this new era. Yesterday's gifts can help us resuscitate today's song of the people.

A new wave of worship is coming in which we incorporate the gifts of the 1970s and 80s into the cornucopia of the banqueting table God has given us in the 2000s. When the songs of the decades come together, the mix will be explosive.

Singing Past the Song

How can we recover and awaken the song of the people? The answer to that question is larger than this book and will unfold in the days to come, but let me use this chapter to at least launch the conversation. For starters, let's teach God's people to *sing past the song*. I'll explain what I mean.

In many churches, people will sing only as long as a known song is being sung by the worship band. We've become platform-dependent—that is, if they don't supply a song, we have nothing to sing. Once the platform's prepared song is finished, the worship of the people is finished. When the known song is done, the people have no more song. Take the lyrics off the screen, and you silence the voices.

It's almost as though our worship is only song deep. When the song is over, the worship stops. God's people need to be taught and trained to sing past the song. After all, when the song stopped, our love didn't stop.

This trend almost resembles Hallmark-card worship. The lyrics on the screen resemble the refined poetry of a Hallmark card. Worshipers sing the lyrics of the Hallmark card to God with passion and sincerity, but then when the lyrics of the card come to an end, the singing also ends. It's as though we don't know how to sing our love to Jesus in words that originate from our own hearts. We're dependent on today's songwriters to give us words so we can worship.

In the past couple decades, we've labored to raise up songwriters who can give us Hallmark-card-quality lyrics in their songs. In the next wave of worship, we're going to labor to help believers sing their own song to the Lord.

The song of the people is not dependent upon the lyrics of known songs and hymns. The song of the people is self-generating, and it comes from the hearts of fire-brands who have been awakened by the cross to the love of Jesus. With nails and thorns before them, their hearts burn with affection for the Son of God. Their eyes are on Jesus, they're beholding the King in His beauty, and they can't help but lift their song to the Lamb (because worship is your first response when you see God).

These burning ones can't be stopped when the song is over. The song of the platform might be over, but not the song of the people. The people have found liberty and confidence to sing past the song. When the platform is finished with its song, the people continue with their own song.

They might sing in the Spirit; they might sing in their native language (such as English); they might sing in other tongues (*glossolalia*); or they might sing from the Psalms or from other Scriptures (see 1 Cor. 14:15; Eph. 5:19; Col. 3:16). There are no boundaries on how the song of the people might be expressed. It's a song of vibrant love for Jesus, and it can be expressed in any way that the Holy Spirit leads.

In the next wave, worship ministries are going to help believers learn how to sing past the song.

Revival

What will awaken the song of the people in these coming days? *Revival!*

The revivals of history have always been characterized by a marked resurgence of the song of the people.

What is revival? To answer that, let me borrow a definition I heard once from Banning Liebscher:

> Revival is a move of the Spirit of God, marked by the Presence and power of God, that awakens the Church to a greater passion for Jesus and His cause in the earth, to see culture transformed and the lost saved.

Almost without exception, God has used new songs in historic revivals to release the song of the people and give the saints language for their newfound joy in the Holy Spirit. In fact, many revivals are associated with the names of two people—the primary apostolic preacher in the revival and the primary worship leader or songwriter in that revival. Let me cite a few examples of these pairings.

John Wesley's ministry was complemented by the songwriting ministry of his brother, Charles Wesley. One of the most remarkable earmarks of the Wesleyan revival was the release of the song of the people. Charles Wesley wrote around 6,500 hymns, providing the Methodist movement with vocabulary to extol the works of God in their midst.

Billy Sunday's evangelistic ministry was supported by song leader and music director Homer Rodeheaver.

The impact of Dwight L. Moody's outreaches was strengthened by the ministry of song leader, songwriter, and soloist Ira D. Sankey.

The Azusa Street revival in Los Angeles (1906–1915) had preacher William Seymore at its center, but no particular song leader. Even so, that revival was characterized by the impassioned song of the people. Some of the favorite songs of The Mission on Azusa Street were "The Comforter Has Come"; "Are You Washed in the Blood?"; "Oh, the Blood of Jesus"; "Under the Blood"; "This Is Like Heaven to Me"; "Where Jesus Is, 'Tis Heaven There"; "The Name of Jesus Is So Sweet"; and "Oh, How I Love Jesus." At the revival's inception, all singing was a cappella and was entirely vocally driven—it was the song of the people. "Singing in tongues" together was also commonly practiced.

The Welch Revival under Evan Roberts saw a notable upsurge of the song of the people. The songs of the meetings weren't initiated by a song leader on a platform, but they came extemporaneously from the crowd. The energy in the people's singing was so riveting that it was one of the features often covered by newspaper journalists. The meetings flowed freely between prayer, song, and preaching.

The Charismatic movement that launched around 1967 was somewhat unique in that it had *many* well-known preachers (rather than a single, central figure), and was facilitated by many songwriters and song leaders. As already described in chapter three, the movement was most widely recognized by the way it ignited the song of the people. Congregations would sing in the Spirit for sustained lengths of time, with the energy for the singing coming entirely from the people, not from musical instruments.

The song of the people. Revival. There you have it. Seemingly without exception, revivals have always been accompanied by mass water baptisms, fiery prayer meetings, and the song of the people.

If we're heading for a resurgence of the song of the people, then I'm going to declare it boldly: *We're heading for revival!* Watch for a great wave of revival in the coming days that will awaken the Church and restore the song of the people.

What else will awaken the song of the people? Signs and wonders.

Signs and Wonders

Signs and wonders are catalytic to releasing the song of the people. Why? Because when we see God moving in our midst in power and glory, we can't help but lift our voices and celebrate God's manifest Presence among us.

This is the kind of worship that swept the crowds during Jesus' triumphal entry into Jerusalem. In his record of that event, Luke connected their lifted voices with signs and wonders:

> *Then, as He was now drawing near the descent of the Mount of Olives, the whole multitude of the disciples began to rejoice and praise God with a loud voice for all the mighty works they had seen, saying: "'Blessed is the King who comes in the name of the Lord!' Peace in heaven and glory in the highest!" And some of the Pharisees called to Him from the crowd, "Teacher, rebuke Your disciples." But He answered and said to them, "I tell you that if these should keep silent, the stones would immediately cry out"* (Luke 19:37–40).

The triumphal entry was an eruption of the song of the people. Their fire was fueled by the mighty works Jesus had done in their midst—signs, wonders, healings, and miracles.

When I look ahead, therefore, to where we're going in worship, I see a dramatic release of Holy Spirit power in which cancers disappear, blind eyes open, demons are cast out, paralytics come out of their wheelchairs, and mental illness is healed instantaneously.

The psalmist wrote, *"Blessed are the people who know the joyful sound! They walk, O Lord, in the light of Your countenance"* (Ps. 89:15). What is *the joyful sound?* It's the sound of praise that will be heard when God turns the light of His countenance toward His people and demonstrates His power in signs, wonders, and healing. When those with congenital disabilities who have never seen or heard anything from birth are suddenly able to see, hear, and speak, a joyful sound of praise will erupt from God's people that will shake the cities of the earth—in the same way the praise of the triumphal entry moved the entire city of Jerusalem (see Matt. 21:10).

The realm of miracles and healing is the domain of worship ministries. Worship leaders, never relax or relent until signs and wonders are happening in your worship services.

Let me repeat where I see this thing going. God is going to visit His Church powerfully in signs and wonders which will release the song of the people.

Released by the Platform

I'm declaring that a day is coming in which the impetus for congregational worship is going to come as much from the congregation as it does from the platform. To get there, our worship ministries must gain a vision for unlocking the song of the people. I envision the day when the platform and congregation function more like antiphonal choirs. Rather than the platform being the initiators and the congregation the responders, I see initiation and response passing antiphonally between them.

The purpose of our worship ministries is not to overpower, replace, out-sing, or drown the song of the people; rather, our purpose is to enable, enhance, inspire, and release the song of the people. But if we're not sufficiently attentive, the electronic power of our sound systems can undermine our objective.

We don't want the trappings and accessories of our worship carts (such as technology, new songs, and powerful equipment, as discussed in chapter nine) to replace the song of the people; rather, we want to steward the abundance of useful tools we've been given so we can support and release the heartfelt praises of God's people.

We've given our worship ministries a vision for starting a *bonfire* on the platform, and I love it when they're able to do that. But there's more. Worship ministries are now gaining a vision for releasing a *forest fire* in the congregation.

Worship leaders, let's ask the Holy Spirit to give us practical keys for unlocking the song of the people. These keys will help us mount the next waves of worship that are coming.

Warfare Praise

To enter into corporate warfare through praise, we must recover the song of the people.

We know from passages such as Second Chronicles 20 that there's a place for corporate spiritual warfare in worship.[1] A local church is an outpost for the Kingdom of God in its region, and it engages the dark powers of a city by spreading light and truth. When a church encounters spiritual warfare in its region, one of its responses is to declare the authority and reign of Christ through praise. Jesus said, *"All authority has been given to Me in heaven and on earth,"* and John called Him *"the ruler over the kings of the earth"* (Matt. 28:18; Rev. 1:5). Therefore, when we extol the authority and power of Christ in our praises, we're serving notice to the powers of darkness that Jesus is Lord in our city.

This kind of praise is bold and fiery. It asserts that we surrender to the Lordship of Christ and resist the powers of darkness in our region. We're laboring for the light and truth of Christ to capture the hearts of men and women whose minds have been darkened by the deceiver's lies (see 2 Cor. 4:4; Eph. 4:18; 2 Tim. 2:26). In the next wave of worship, churches are going to rise to their role of declaring the praises of God in their region. This sound will go forth as the song of the people.

There's a time for everything, so there's a time for every form of praise and worship (see Eccl. 3:7). There's a time for quiet contemplation, a time for intimate communion with Jesus, and also a time for full-throated exaltation. Exaltation, adoration, and celebration are probably the mainstay of corporate worship. In contrast, warfare in worship is likely to be rarer in its occurrence.

However, in those unique moments when the Holy Spirit inspires militancy in our praise, let's be ready to catch that wave. Psalm 66:8 seems to support this kind of full-throated praise: *"Make the voice of His praise to be heard."*

Jesus, awaken the song of Your people so that we can catch every wave of the Spirit in this hour!

An Interactive Encounter

The next wave of worship will focus primarily in two directions: vertical worship and horizontal worship. In corporate worship, the focus of worship is mostly *up* and *around*. Let me explain my meaning.

By *vertical worship*, I mean an intimate and whole-hearted preoccupation with the person of Christ. In vertical worship, all eyes are on our magnificent obsession, the Lord Jesus Himself. The Body of Christ has awakened to vertical worship in fantastic ways in the past thirty years with a keynote emphasis on intimacy with Jesus. Ministries such as Bethel Music and the International House of Prayer have played a significant role in helping us forward in this emphasis on intimate devotion to Jesus.

Some groups in the Body of Christ have excelled at *horizontal worship*, meaning the interactive dynamics of worship that happen among worshipers who are gathered together in one place to lift up the name of Jesus. From the window of my personal experience, African and African

American churches have led this charge. They've shown us how to have a praise party *together*. The Africans, as well as the Hispanics, have touched something here that is going to infect the global Church. Their contribution is going to help us keep moving forward because interactive worship is dynamically helpful in releasing the song of the people.

If you want to go quiet, internal, and contemplative, your best place for that is your secret place. If you want to go interactive and vertical where the song of the people crescendos, go to the congregation.

A wave of worship is coming in which we're going to explore both the vertical and interactive dimensions of worship. The synergy of the two will release the song of the people.

Songs of the Nations

Isaiah prophesied that at the end of the age songs would arise from all the nations of the earth (see Isa. 24:14–16; 26:1–2; 42:10–12). As the song of the people is released, the songs of the nations will gain an international platform, especially through YouTube, Vimeo, and similar digital platforms.

At the time of this writing, it's most common for international worship hits to originate from English-speaking nations such as the United States, Canada, England, South Africa, Australia, New Zealand, etc. But some of the songs in the next wave of worship will be written initially in other languages—such as Spanish, French, German, Russian, Korean, Chinese, Portuguese, Hindi, Arabic, Hebrew, Swahili, etc.—and then will be translated into the international language of English and broadcast worldwide.

Watch for Africa—new songs and sounds of worship are going to come out of Africa.

Also, I'm looking for powerful songs to come out of nations where believers are persecuted for their faith. What kinds of dangerous songs might the Holy Spirit give us from prisons of persecution?

Furthermore, the songs of the next Holy Spirit waves will come in a wide variety of musical genres. The creatives will help us with this. We'll revel in the goodness of Jesus to the accompaniment of musical genres such as hip hop, rhythm and blues, reggae, country, classical, rock, jazz, funk, techno, swing, Indie, ska, salsa, bossa nova, musical theatre, and gospel. God is always creatively unpredictable, so why should we get stuck in one genre? You can catch some great waves in the fusion of different genres.

Just like heaven, worship is going more international than ever.

Worshipers and Watchers

Some are worshipers, and some are watchers. This reminds me of David and his wife, Michal. When David escorted the ark of the Lord's Presence into Jerusalem, Michal watched from a window while David worshiped. Every worship service seems to have two groups: the worshipers and the watchers.

Now, I'm not critical of the fact that people come to our services to watch our worship. Quite the opposite! I *love* the fact that our churches are filled with watchers. I could wish that the *whole world* would come to our churches and watch the praises of our King. If they would come and watch, perhaps they would eventually worship. And that's precisely what our souls long for—that millions would come and watch, and then be drawn to worship. We want our worship houses *filled* with watchers—we just don't want them to *remain* watchers. We want to draw people forward in grace so that the watchers become worshipers. We'll never relent until every creature in heaven, and on the earth, and under the earth is lifting high the name of Jesus.

When John saw the worship of heaven, he wasn't shown a platform or stage. Rather, he saw a vast multitude of living creatures, elders, angels, humans, and every imaginable kind of creature lifting their voices in praise to the Lamb (see Rev. 4–5).

Worship in this new era will not be moving toward a greater platform presence, but a greater release of the multitude. The Lamb deserves the song of every creature!

Questions for Wave Riders:

1. What can worship ministries do to release the song of the people?

2. Is your church exercised in singing past the song? How could your church grow in this grace?

3. Talk about the connection between revival and the song of the people. What's your vision for revival?

4. How can our worship ministries gain a greater vision for igniting a forest fire in the congregation?

5. What is the role of warfare through praise in the coming days?

Note

1. For a fuller biblical understanding of praise in spiritual warfare, see chapter three in my book *Exploring Worship: A Practical Guide to Praise and Worship*.

Chapter 11

Lamb-Centric Worship

WORSHIP ALWAYS HAS been and always will be about Jesus. Let me state the obvious: *The next wave of worship is going to be fixed primarily on the Lord Jesus Christ.* That's not a prophetic prediction; it's simply an acknowledgment that worship has always flourished when it has returned its focus to the centrality of Christ. For two thousand years, the Church has been prone to wander and has returned, over and over, to the centrality of Christ.

But let me be even more specific. The next wave of worship is going to center primarily around Jesus the *Lamb of God.* I'm making that assertion because Scripture reveals that's where worship is ultimately headed.

When we need the vitality of our worship to be renewed, where should we go? Back to the beginning. Where did it all start? Well, if you follow the river of worship all the way back to its headwaters, you'll be standing at the foot of the cross.

Christ crucified is the source, inspiration, and fountainhead of worship. That's where the two of you first met. You'll recover your first love by returning to the place where your love was first kindled (see Rev. 2:4). With every return visit, you excavate love's passions and redig the wells of gratefulness, abandonment, and loyalty.

The cross is the alpha and omega of worship—that is, it's where worship both starts and ends. When I say worship ends with the cross, I have an end-time meaning in mind. When John saw worship at the end of the age, he saw all creation gathered around *the Lamb*. With every eye fixated on Him, every creature was saying, *"Worthy is the Lamb who was slain to receive power and riches and wisdom, and strength and honor and glory and blessing!"* (Rev. 5:12).

Like many things, worship has a tendency to get weird and imbalanced. All too easily, congregational worship can become about music, platforms, screens, lights, careers, screenshots, profiles, egos, and income streams. The whole thing must get calibrated, over and over, to the cross—where all the accoutrements fall away and our gaze remains on only one thing—*"a Lamb as though it had been slain"* (Rev. 5:6).

Jesus is the magnificent Lion of the tribe of Judah, and we're going to worship the Lion forever! And yet, when John beheld heaven's worship, the focus was on Jesus the Lamb. What the Lamb of God sacrificed for us is so compelling that it will occupy our praises for eternity. Calvary opened an eternal fountain, and our romantic obsession with the Lamb will carry our love forever.

Sometimes worship leaders struggle to find corporate momentum in the Spirit when leading a congregation in worship. When they ask me what to do, my answer is usually, *Take us back to the cross*. That's where tears flow, hearts warm, and spirits soar. The cross lifts every head, every eye, and every heart. It's the genesis and fountainhead of love—an inexhaustible treasure trove for the language of love. A return to the cross opens unquenchable fires and unending love songs.

Songwriters, you're going to write your best love songs by stationing at the cross. Here, love inspires love; abandonment empowers abandonment; longing fuels longing; zeal ignites zeal; deeps calls unto deep; tears beget tears. The best songs about the cross have yet to be written.

Stop once more and behold your crucified Savior. Gaze on His hands, feet, brow, and pierced side. Whisper your gratitude, and let the fountains of affection flow.

The Lord's Table

In the next wave of worship, I'm expecting a renewed appreciation for the Lord's Table. When He instituted this Supper, Jesus placed it at the center of our worship and commanded us to remember His death until He comes (see 1 Cor. 11:23–26). Its visibility in worship is going to increase as we approach the return of Christ.

I grew up in a church tradition in which Communion was celebrated less frequently than in the more historic churches. In fact, I can remember thinking that Communion was sometimes a distraction from worship, or even a detraction from worship, because I thought it used up precious service time that could have otherwise been given to singing. But now, because of the Lord's gentle corrections, I'm asking Him for greater revelation into the riches He's provided for us in this Table.

The Lord's Supper has the potential to deepen worship and awaken love, and I encourage every leader reading this to pursue that potential aggressively. Do it more frequently, and plan for it more intentionally. The cross is the power of our Gospel (see 1 Cor. 1:22–24), and power is made available to us through His Table.

One way to pursue the powerful potential in receiving Christ's body and blood is by doing it differently each time, even in the smallest ways. Surf the waves of the Spirit even in the way you serve Communion. Search for ways to introduce greater creativity and diversity into this holy celebration:

- Use a wide variety of Scriptures in directing our meditation to the Supper. Draw literally from Genesis to Revelation. Don't recite the same portion of Scripture in a rote manner every time, but look for biblical texts that bring fresh light and meaning to the celebration.

- Place the Supper at different points in the service order. Start a service with it, or end a service with it. Do it after the first song, or after the second, or during the third song, or during the fourth song. Let it be part of the altar call. Or pair it up with the offering.

- In one service, serve everyone; in another service, make it optional for those who want to help themselves. Allow servers to bring it to the people in one setting, and then invite the people to approach the servers in another setting.

Serve it during singing; serve it during silence; serve it while a special song is being performed; serve it during a water baptism service.

Sometimes worship becomes me-centered; that is, we easily become preoccupied with our own thoughts and feelings in His Presence. The Lord's Table can help to keep our worship Christ-centered.

I want to catch a wave of worship in which the cross of Christ is front and center, and the hope of our Gospel rivets and wins the hearts of this generation.

Release of Worship Shepherds

I can suppose a worship leader responding by saying, "My church doesn't allow me to officiate Communion. The only thing I'm empowered to do in worship is lead singing."

I see a wave of worship coming in which we take the constraints off our worship ministries. When we allow worship teams only to lead songs, we clip their wings and hinder their effectiveness. Not all waves of worship can be mounted simply by singing a song. Sometimes something else is necessary in order to unlock the moment and find the wave's sweet spot.

Jesus said He would give us the keys of the Kingdom, and we need those Kingdom keys in order to open the potential of worship services. Sometimes it takes a specific key to open a worship service, and we want to enable worship teams to use a diversity of Kingdom keys in our services.

Worship leaders are shepherds. We guide the flock, taking them to green pastures and quiet waters. We serve the entire person. We don't only serve them when they're singing, but during every step of their journey as they take up their cross and follow Jesus.

In the next wave of worship, we'll do well to allow our worship ministries to do whatever they need to do to find the sweet spot on the wave, and then take it all the way to the shore.

I see waves of worship in which worship teams are released, according to the leading of the Holy Spirit, to do things such as:

- lead in singing;

- lead in prayer;

- initiate Communion;

- invite people to receive personal ministry for healing and deliverance;

- call for people to repent, or commit their lives to Christ;

- invite people to receive anointing with oil and the laying on of hands;

- prophesy to them for their edification;

- exhort the congregation from Scripture;

- read Scripture;

- coach the congregation in the singing of Scripture;

- invite people to pray together for one another;

- receive an offering as an expression of worship;

- make room for the gifts of the Spirit to be exercised (see 1 Cor. 12:8–10); and

- invite people to bow in reverence before the Lord.

As a psalmist, David ministered under a powerful prophetic anointing, and today's psalmists are searching for those waters. My friend Chris Tofilon told me he sees a wave in worship coming in which psalmists with a John the Baptist anointing will call out the brood of vipers so they'll want to kill the guy. That would be an undomesticated wave!

When we open to more than just the singing of songs in our worship services, how can we know when we did something that was according to the leading of the Holy Spirit? Let me suggest this litmus test: We judge something as valid and Spirit-led when it adds to the spirit of worship in the meeting. This is the principle of 1 Corinthians 14:5, *"that the church may receive edification."* If the entire church was edified, or if the water level of the meeting was raised, it was fittingly expressed. But if someone's contribution deflates the spirit of worship in the meeting, they should be teachable and eager to learn from the incident.

Worship is so much more than just singing, and we'll have a better chance of catching the coming waves of the Spirit and remain Lamb-centered if we're free to do more in our worship services than just sing songs.

Sprinkling of Blood

Worship teams usually prepare vigorously for corporate worship, so when the church gathers, they're ready to go.

And off they go! But most believers attending the meeting have not exercised the same careful preparation, and they often come to the meeting soiled from living in this world.

In the next wave of worship, worship teams are going to be more intentional about preparing people for the privilege of entering the Lord's gates.

When we gather to worship, most of us hear two voices in our ears. In one ear, we hear the voice of the accuser. Satan accuses us whenever we attempt to draw close to God (see Rev. 12:10–11). He tries to convince us we're not worthy to approach God's holiness. His scheme is to separate us from the Father's embrace and isolate us so he can devour us.

What should we do about this? The passage gives the answer: *"And they overcame him by the blood of the Lamb"* (Rev. 12:11). We overcome the accuser by using the blood.

In the other ear, we hear another voice—the voice of our conscience. God has given us a conscience for redemptive reasons, but sometimes it gets hyperactive. Where satan stops accusing, our conscience often picks it up and condemns us for our poor performance as a Christian.

I know the answer to both the voice of our conscience and the voice of satan's accusations. What's the answer? The blood of Christ. Jesus shed His blood on Calvary so we could be cleansed, made righteous and holy, and be qualified by grace to draw near to God and His majestic Holiness.

The cleansing we can receive from Christ's blood is called, in the New Testament, the *sprinkling of blood* (see 1 Pet. 1:2; Heb. 12:24). Hebrews 10:19–22 is my favorite passage for this:

> *Therefore, brethren, having boldness to enter the Holiest by the blood of Jesus, by a new and living way which He consecrated for us, through the veil, that is, His flesh, and having a High Priest over the house of God, let us draw near with a true heart in full assurance of faith, having our hearts sprinkled from an evil conscience and our bodies washed with pure water.*

This passage is so precious to me that I invoke the sprinkling of blood over my life every day. It's part of my morning shower routine.[1] Whenever I enter a worship service, therefore, I enter with boldness and confidence because my conscience is already sprinkled by the blood of Christ.

But many saints haven't yet learned they can be sprinkled daily with the blood of Christ on their conscience. Consequently, when they step into a worship service, they're still hearing the two voices in their ears. In one ear, they're hearing satan's accusations; in the other, they're hearing the condemning voice of their conscience.

Right now, most worship teams launch into a worship set without giving much regard to the voices of accusation and condemnation that harass many believers. It's difficult to catch a wave of worship when the congregation feels like they're drowning in accusation.

In the next wave of worship, worship ministries will help believers access the power of Christ's sprinkled blood. We're going to slow down and help believers prepare their hearts for worship by receiving the cleansing of Christ's blood. Under the blood, we enter the Holiest with boldness!

The next wave will see the Body of Christ passionately worshiping the Lamb of God with boldness and confidence because of the power of Christ's blood.

The Fear of the Lord

The cleansing of Christ's precious blood gives us boldness to draw near to God, and it does something else as well—it fuels the fear of the Lord. In his First Epistle, Peter connected the cleansing of Christ's blood to the fear of the Lord (1 Pet. 1:17–19). Why would our honoring of the blood of the Lamb cause us to fear? Because of the magnitude of the sacrifice that gave us this cleansing.

Jesus' blood was shed at a great price! Having received such a great gift, we're now stewards of this trust. And stewards are accountable. Peter saw it as a fearful thing that we're accountable to God for how we steward the blood of the Lamb.

Worship and the fear of the Lord have kissed. Their shared history in Scripture is beautiful. (For example, see Gen. 22:12; 2 Kings 17:36; Ps. 5:7; Rev. 14:7; 15:4). In the oldest song recorded in Scripture, the seraphim cry, "Holy, holy, holy!" as they worship forever in the midst of lightning and thunder (Isa. 6:3; Rev. 4:8). The closer you get to God, the more encounters you'll have with the fear of the Lord (see Heb. 12:21).

The true fear of the Lord, properly understood, doesn't cause us to pull away but lean forward into His Presence. Never fear the fear of the Lord! Run into it, and wrap your arms around it.

If God fears God, how much more should we (see Heb. 5:7; Isa. 11:2)?

How might we define the fear of the Lord? *A trembling zeal to obey every word of His mouth* (see Isa. 50:10; 66:2; Ps. 112:1).

In the coming waves of worship, I foresee corporate encounters with the fear of the Lord. Watch for waves that level us in His Presence and leave us trembling in reverential awe under the weight of His Glory.

Questions for Wave Riders:

1. Talk about the centrality of the cross to worship. In what ways do we tend to move off center?

2. What role do you see the Lord's Table playing in the coming wave of worship?

3. Do you think worship teams should be limited only to leading in songs? Why or why not?

4. What can we do to help believers gain greater confidence in drawing near to God in worship?

Note

1. My book *Power of the Blood* expands on this idea.

Chapter 12

PROPHETIC SPONTANEITY

IN THE NEXT wave of worship, watch for greater spontaneity in our expressions of love and for an even stronger prophetic flow in worship. Let me unpack what I mean.

Paul divided the songs we sing into three categories—psalms, hymns, and spiritual songs:

> *Speaking to one another in psalms and hymns and spiritual songs, singing and making melody in your heart to the Lord* (Ephesians 5:19).
>
> *Let the word of Christ dwell in you richly in all wisdom, teaching and admonishing one another in psalms and hymns and spiritual songs, singing with grace in your hearts to the Lord* (Colossians 3:16).

Let me explain what Paul meant by these three designations.

By *psalms,* Paul meant the singing of Scripture. The book of Psalms is the Bible's songbook, so it's the most commonly sung portion of Scripture but not the only one. We also sing from virtually *all* the books of the Bible.

By *hymns,* Paul meant songs of human composition. The lyrics aren't taken verbatim from Scripture, but they support biblical ideas and glorify Jesus. When we sing the latest YouTube worship hits, we're singing hymns. Most songs being written and sung today would properly be called *hymns* (as Paul used the term).

And by *spiritual songs,* Paul meant the spontaneous singing of songs that are moved along by the waves of the Holy Spirit. The words of a spiritual song don't come directly from a Scripture or from the lyrics of a composed hymn but come straight from a worshiper's heart as they express their thoughts to Jesus in the moment. Spiritual songs are unpremeditated, spontaneous, extemporaneous, and unrehearsed. Spiritual songs can be sung in other tongues as the Spirit gives utterance or can be sung in a person's native tongue (such as English or Spanish) (see Acts 2:4; 1 Cor. 14:15).

When we see that Scripture has sanctioned a wide variety of song, from psalms and hymns to spiritual songs, we realize we've been empowered in the Spirit to capture all the waves of worship He's going to be sending.

In the 1960s, all the churches were singing hymns only. In the 1970s, the Holy Spirit taught the Body of

Christ to sing spiritual songs. Then, in the 2000s, the Church began to explore the singing of Scripture in a more intentional way.

At the time of this writing, most churches on the earth devote almost the entirety of their corporate worship to the singing of hymns (songs of human composition). We're a bit stuck in a hymn-dominant worship culture right now, but the Lord is going to continue to draw us forward. In the waves of worship that are coming, watch for a more equal distribution between all three of Paul's song expressions—psalms, hymns, and spiritual songs. Get ready for that wave because it's going to be great!

24/7 Worship

In 1999, a 24/7 worship-and-prayer ministry called The International House of Prayer launched in Kansas City, Missouri. Since its inception, this house of prayer has conducted worship-infused intercessory prayer meetings nonstop, 365 days a year. Worship teams alternate in leading two-hour prayer sets round the clock. The live webstream is followed around the world (see ihopkc.org).

Affectionately called IHOP, this ministry is making profound contributions to the worship movement particularly in three ways:

- They're inspiring 24/7 worship around the globe simply by the fact that they're doing it.

- They're modeling how to combine music with prayer to make intercession joyful and enjoyable, according to Isaiah's prophecy, *"Even them I will bring to My holy mountain, and make them joyful in My house of prayer. Their burnt offerings and their sacrifices will be accepted on My altar; for My house shall be called a house of prayer for all nations"* (Isa. 56:7).

- They're exploring and inspiring the singing of Scripture more extensively and aggressively than possibly any other ministry on the earth. Because of their example, worship ministries on every continent are following their model of singing Scripture.

Due in part to IHOP's example, some worship teams in the Body of Christ today sing psalms from the Scriptures in public contexts. For example, some singers will take a passage of Scripture and sing their way through the passage, in psalm fashion, for all in the room to hear. But this practice has not yet worked its way into the worship vocabulary of your typical congregation. It's rare to find a local church that practices the corporate singing of Scripture. But it's coming. A wave of worship is coming in which entire congregations will freely sing from Scripture together.

How might this be expressed? I foresee believers bringing their Bibles to worship services and loving Jesus in the worship service by singing a verse that's laid open in their hands. I also see churches placing a dedicated screen in their sanctuaries where the only thing projected on that screen will be Scriptures for the people to pray and sing.

When psalms, hymns, and spiritual songs are used together, they become a combustive mix to ignite 24/7 worship. In the coming waves of the Holy Spirit, worship won't be confined to thirty vibrant minutes in a public gathering. Rather, worship will translate into a fiery 24/7 reality in the hearts of God's people. Worship ministries will not focus merely on crafting a 30-minute worship experience on a Sunday morning, but will focus on equipping the Body of Christ for 24/7 worship before the throne of God.

Thematic Diversity

When we intentionally incorporate psalms, hymns, and spiritual songs into our corporate worship services, something else happens: The breadth of our vocabulary expands, which in turn makes worship richer and deeper.

A wave of worship is coming in which our vocabulary of worship will diversify and reflect the themes of the *whole* counsel of God: the Kingdom, salvation, Holy Spirit power, sanctification, obedience, suffering, intimacy, end times, identity, family, judgment, grace, redemption, intercession, courage, faith, mercy, revival, the beauty of Jesus, the blood, brokenness, compassion, discipleship, endurance, giving, heaven, the Trinity, knowing God, love, evangelism, persecution, Communion, servanthood, forgiveness, sovereignty, waiting on God, and more.

As my friend Ruben Cervantes observed, we need to introduce theology back into the songs we sing. We need songs that teach because church culture is shaped by the theology we sing.

Songs, hymns, and spiritual songs will help us explore *all* the themes of the Kingdom in our worship.

The Creatives

In the next wave, we're going to worship Jesus through a greater diversity in the arts. Get ready because the creatives are coming. Who are they? Those in the Body of Christ with a holy anointing to harness the latest technologies and release creativity in the proclamation of psalms, hymns, and spiritual songs.

We will see increasing creativity in the use of *film* in worship in the coming decades. The Scriptures draw a strong connection between worship and the eyes, and the creatives will help us explore that holy ground. We've seen YouTube explode as a visual medium for worship, but we're just at the beginning of this wave. Online platforms such as YouTube will continue to be used creatively to spread psalms, hymns, and spiritual songs throughout the earth.

Spontaneity

When we're equipped to sing all three song forms—psalms, hymns, and spiritual songs—the potential for spontaneity in worship multiplies. Spontaneity naturally follows when we feel permission to practice all three in corporate worship.

Let me identify what spontaneous worship is. Spontaneous worship is the freedom to move seamlessly between psalms, hymns, and spiritual songs as the Holy Spirit leads.

Whenever the topic of spontaneity in worship comes up, we immediately feel the familiar tension between spontaneity and preparation. Some folks think spontaneity happens when we scrap the idea of preparing for worship and just show up and see where the Spirit might lead.

Where no preparation has been invested into worship, you end up with aimlessness not spontaneity.

Preparation and spontaneity are fast friends. Preparation empowers spontaneity. Preparation provides a safety net that gives you courage to deviate from your preparation. When you're prepared with a worship set list, you can follow a spontaneous prompting with courage because you know you can always return to your set list.

The more spontaneous you want to be, the harder you must work to prepare.

Labor hard to plan for worship but then hold your preparation lightly because now you'll enjoy the freedom of moving seamlessly between psalms, hymns, and spiritual songs.

The next wave of worship will be less weighted toward the curated and more courageous in the spontaneous.

Prophetic Worship

Earlier I referenced *prophetic flow in worship*, and I want to explain my meaning. There's a symbiotic relationship between worship and prophecy, and David set a precedent by exploring it aggressively.

More specifically, David and his military cabinet appointed musical Levites *"who should prophesy with harps, stringed instruments, and cymbals"* (1 Chron. 25:1). The passage says they were the ones *"who prophesied with a harp to give thanks and to praise the Lord"* (v. 3). Their thanks and praise flowed like inspired oracles.

Were they prophesying while musical instruments were being played? Or was the very playing of their instruments an expression of prophecy? *Both*. They sang prophecies, and they also prophesied upon their instruments. Musicians can prophesy, therefore, with their voices and also with their instruments.[1]

How does prophesying on an instrument work? When musicians are sensitive to the leading of the Holy Spirit, they can play their instrument in a way that opens the hearts of the congregation to more of God.

An anointed musical interlude, played spontaneously in the Spirit at a strategic moment, can sometimes carry more impact than spoken or sung words. I've been in services where a drummer played an unexpected drum solo in such a Spirit-inspired way that it broke the meeting open.

There are moments in worship when it's fitting for an anointed guitarist to take off on a screaming lead guitar solo in prophetic joy. There are other moments when it's fitting for a sax or flute player to feel their way on the waves of the Spirit.

In the coming wave of worship, I see musicians prophesying on their instruments and singers singing prophetic oracles of praise spontaneously as the Holy Spirit gives utterance.

I love how Paul described the way prophecy can work in a public worship gathering:

> *But if all prophesy, and an unbeliever or an uninformed person comes in, he is convinced by all, he is convicted by all. And thus the secrets of*

his heart are revealed; and so, falling down on his face, he will worship God and report that God is truly among you (1 Corinthians 14:25).

In context, Paul was addressing proper order in corporate worship gatherings. He said that, when the Spirit of God moves in corporate worship, a prophetic spirit can fall on the meeting. As the gift of prophecy is expressed, God reads the mail of an unbeliever in the meeting. He's not embarrassed by the prophecy that's given, but he realizes that God sees him, knows him, and recognizes the longings of his heart.

When the secret desires of his heart are revealed, Paul said he will fall on his face, worship God, and then go and tell his friends, "God is with those people."

Isn't this what we want? We want such a strong reality of God's Presence in our midst that *unbelievers* are falling on their faces in our worship services and declaring that God is among us.[2]

I see a prophetic wave of worship coming that is so strong it sweeps unbelievers off their feet and levels them with the realization that God is among His people.

Questions for Wave Riders:

1. What can our churches do to have a stronger representation of all three song forms—psalms, hymns, and spiritual songs—in our meetings?

2. *The creatives are coming.* What does that statement mean to you?

3. Talk about Bob's definition of spontaneous worship. How was that helpful to you?

4. *Worship ministries will not focus merely on crafting a 30-minute worship experience on a Sunday morning, but will focus on equipping the Body of Christ for 24/7 worship before the throne of God.* Do you share this vision? Why or why not?

Notes

1. For further study on this theme, see chapter seven in my book *Exploring Worship: A Practical Guide to Praise and Worship.*

2. For more on this, see my book *Following the River: A Vision for Corporate Worship.*

Chapter 13

ANCIENT PATHS

TO PARTICIPATE IN God's next wave of worship, we must look forward to the new and also look back to the ancient.

First, we must look forward to the new because God is always doing new things, as He said: *"Behold, I will do a new thing, now it shall spring forth; shall you not know it?"* (Isa. 43:19). As you read the ocean, look for new things in worship that history has never seen before.

At the same time, look back at the ancient ways of God because He is unchanging and everything He does is consistent with all He has ever done. In fact, He specifically calls us to the ancient:

> *Thus says the Lord: "Stand in the ways and see, and ask for the old paths, where the good way is, and walk in it; then you will find rest for your souls"* (Jeremiah 6:16).

Because My people have forgotten Me, they have burned incense to worthless idols. And they have caused themselves to stumble in their ways, from the ancient paths, to walk in pathways and not on a highway (18:15).

The Lord has called us to *ancient paths*. Ancient paths lead to ancient anointings. I heard David Demian say in a Zoom session that God is releasing ancient anointings for end-time purposes.

To discern the new, you must be living in the ancient. Jesus said the wise will value both new and old:

Therefore every scribe instructed concerning the kingdom of heaven is like a householder who brings out of his treasure things new and old (Matthew 13:52).

This book is focused mostly on looking forward to the new, but in this chapter let's look back to the ancient. There are ancient elements in worship that, when honored carefully, will position us for the new waves of the Spirit.

Devotion to Jesus

The bedrock of all worship is a personal, extravagant, lovesick devotion to Jesus. This has always been, and will always be, the foundation of worship. Worship is personal—we're singing to a Man. We don't care if anyone else ever sings our song, just as long as Jesus hears it.

With Paul, we gladly forfeit everything in the abandoned pursuit of just one thing: *"the excellence of the knowledge of Christ Jesus"* (Phil. 3:8). Worshipers aren't into songs or music; we're into Jesus. We want to *"know Him and the power of His resurrection, and the fellowship of His sufferings"* (Phil. 3:10). This ancient pursuit of the face of Christ consumes us in these last days. It's all about love.

My friend psalmist David Forlu told me, "We have a huge responsibility to be people after God's heart who know Him in His fullness. Then He can share His secrets with us and enable us with grace to write songs that change a culture and generation."

Mary Alessi added, "God is taking us back to the place He's always wanted us—knowing Him! All we want is to know Him, more and more, in His character and nature."

My friend psalmist Laura Souguellis from Brazil spoke with me about how the writing of songs has become a formula for success. Songwriters are eager to write popular songs because of the success that attends a worship hit. They go into songwriting mode and work their craft to produce a good song. As a result, Laura said believers find themselves trying to worship with songs that weren't actually birthed out of worship. Rather, they were written in a practice lab in the hope of writing a killer song.

The songs in the next wave of worship will come from a womb of lovesickness where psalmists come aside, return to their first love, and lavish their affection on Jesus.

Getting back to our first love is the ancient way.

Godly Character

For anointing to endure, it must be accompanied by character. We learn this from the tragic example of Samson who was anointed powerfully by the Holy Spirit to accomplish great exploits, but yet suffered great ruin because his character didn't match his anointing.

God wants character in His Levites. We see how important this is to Him in this verse:

> *He will sit as a refiner and a purifier of silver; He will purify the sons of Levi, and purge them as gold and silver, that they may offer to the Lord an offering in righteousness* (Malachi 3:3).

God will purify His Levites until our character reflects His righteousness. His refining fire will burn away impurities so that the gold of Christlikeness shines brightly in our lives. He never asked for an offering in excellence; He asked for an offering in righteousness. In jealousy, He won't relent until His Levites walk in holiness and humility.

The ancient grace of humility is our only way forward in these last days. If it's not bathed in humility, God will resist it. When we catch the next waves of worship, humility is the only thing that will enable us to ride it all the way to the shore. Bow low, and cry out for mercy.

Hype is not humility. Hype demonstrates an intensity that's disproportionate to the reality of the moment. It's hype when a worship leader acts like they're riding the barrel of a wave when, in fact, they're still looking for one.

John the Baptist grew up in the deserts because God wanted his character to match his anointing. At Jesus' baptism, the text gives the impression that no one else but John saw the Dove as it descended on Jesus. To see the Dove, you had to have a John the Baptist lifestyle. Adopt the kind of lifestyle, therefore, that can see the Dove's movements.

The next wave will be captured by Levites who walk in the ancient paths of integrity, truth, humility, and righteousness.

The Cross

I realize I already devoted chapter eleven to the cross, but when speaking of a return to the ancient, I have to repeat myself and say it one more time: *The only way to catch the next wave of worship is by fixating intentionally on the cross and the slain Lamb of Calvary.*

Worship is always a response to revelation, and the cross is the most perfect revelation in all Scripture of who God really is. When we behold the love of God in the cross, therefore, we can't help but soar on the winds of worship.

During his revelation of Christ, John was shown several instances of heavenly worship, and not all were of equal intensity. When I consider which worship moments in Revelation were the most intense, I lean (in my own opinion) toward three instances: Revelation 5:6–14, Revelation 7:9–12, and Revelation 19:6–7.

And what was the central focus on all three occasions? The Lamb of God.

Praise always seeks to match the greatness of the accomplishment. For example, when Steve Jobs died (mastermind and co-founder of Apple Corporation), everyone rose to laud the genius of his accomplishments. Writers and commentators around the world were reaching for language to befit the significance of his legacy. They wanted their praise to properly reflect the impact of his contributions.

In a similar way, when you really see the cross, you reach for praise that rises to the grandeur of Golgotha. A revelation of the Lamb opens the fountains of the highest praise and deepest worship. May we never cease searching for expressions of worship commensurate to the magnificence of Calvary!

I prophesy that an increasing percentage of the new songs that will be written in the coming days are going to point, in some manner, to the cross. It's the only way to capture the wave.

We live in a day when sinister forces within the Church actually work to diminish the centrality of the cross.[1] Never befriend such sentiments and emphases, but instead, make yourself a friend of the cross (see Phil. 3:18). The cross is not our shame but our glory (see Gal. 6:14).

I advocate placing a cross conspicuously in our worship facilities. If it's our center, why not make it the central motif of our décor? May it be the epicenter of our focus, and may it always remind us of why we're here. When we labor to find creative ways to place the cross front and center in both our proclamation and worship, we position ourselves for the sweet spot in the wave.

Pursue innovation in worship by clinging relentlessly to the cross of Christ.

I see a call to the ancient in the lyrics of George Bennard's 1912 hymn, "The Old Rugged Cross":

So I'll cherish the old rugged cross

Till my trophies at last I lay down

I will cling to the old rugged cross

And exchange it some day for a crown.

Singing of Scripture

It bears repeating that the corporate singing of Scripture will be a significant element in enabling us to capture the coming waves of worship.

The singing of Scripture is an ancient practice. Paul wrote about it: *"Let the word of Christ dwell in you richly in all wisdom, teaching and admonishing one another in psalms and hymns and spiritual songs, singing with grace in your hearts to the Lord"* (Col. 3:16). Paul was saying that, as we meditate in the Word day and night and allow His Word to live richly in our hearts, it should naturally be expressed from our lives in song.

Singing Scripture is much more ancient than Paul. For example, David practiced it. He would take his Bible—which was likely composed of Genesis, Exodus, Leviticus, Numbers, Deuteronomy, Joshua, and Judges—place it open on a stand, grab his harp, sit before the ark of the covenant, gaze into the Glory, peer into a verse, and then sing what he read. As he sang the verse, fire would ignite, tears would brim, and love would flow. David knew what it was like to sing just one verse for an hour—singing it from every angle possible—to excavate everything he could find in that Scripture.

I have a theory I can't prove, but I think David's favorite Bible book to sing was Deuteronomy. Why? Because there are certain words in Deuteronomy that appear multiple times in David's psalms.

Deuteronomy called the Lord *our King*, and when you come to David's psalms, you find King, King, King over and over.

In Deuteronomy, God is our shield; in David's psalms, He's our shield, shield, shield.

In Deuteronomy, God is a refuge for us; in David's psalms, He's our refuge, refuge, refuge.

In Deuteronomy, God is our Rock; come to David, and you'll find Rock, Rock, Rock all over his psalms.

David, what are you doing? He's taking one verse, going deep in it, singing it from every angle imaginable, and then writing his psalms from the overflow of the Scripture dwelling in him richly.

Singing Scripture is the ancient way of the psalmists, and it's the way today's psalmists will lead us forward on the coming waves of worship.

The Psalmist Anointing

The psalmist anointing on David was not confined by the Holy Spirit to his generation, but is equally available to worshipers today. Worship leaders, go after the ancient psalmist anointing!

What was the psalmist anointing? It was a Holy Spirit anointing that came upon David in his secret place as he worshiped his beloved Lord. That anointing enabled him to write songs that expressed his cry to God, and then when he shared them with the nation, all of Israel found language for their worship. Furthermore, he entered into the spirit of prophecy and sang of things to come. This same Holy Spirit anointing is available to psalmists today who position themselves for it.

Psalmists go deep and high—that is, they go deep in the Word and high in the Spirit. My best metaphor for this is a kite. When a kite is grounded to the earth, it can soar in the heavens. Similarly, when psalmists are grounded in truth, they can soar on the winds of the Spirit—worship *"in Spirit and truth."* The deeper you go in truth, the higher you can soar in worship.

The psalmist anointing is not primarily a platform anointing, but a secret place anointing. Psalmists are made in secret. They take the fire the Spirit has kindled in their hearts in secret, and then they simply burn in public. The same song that kindled them privately now kindles them publicly. The psalmist anointing isn't something to chase when you're on a platform, but when you're in your secret place. When God does something bright in you in secret, the song will light up the entire house (see Matt. 5:15).

Jesus said, *"I have food to eat of which you do not know"* (John 4:32). In a similar way, psalmists have things going on with Jesus in secret that nobody else knows about. But they're willing to bring some of it to the platform, as the Spirit leads, so that it might bring light to the whole house.

A psalmist's strongest anointing is not on a platform, but in the secret place.

Psalmists learn to buy oil in secret so that, when they're on a platform, they're burning oil and not wick.

Contemporary psalmists under an ancient Davidic anointing will be enabled, by the power of the Holy Spirit, to help us capture the coming waves of worship. Psalmists, go after this oil! Buy it, and do not sell.

Wounded Psalmists

When you meditate in the book of Psalms, you get the impression they were written by people who were wounded by God (see Ps. 69:26). *"Faithful are the wounds of a friend"* (Prov. 27:6). When God wounds His friends, He does it in faithfulness to draw from them the deepest songs.

The ancient paths were walked by psalmists with a limp.

My friend psalmist David Lugo was raised in grinding poverty in Argentina, and then he was hit by a car in a near-death experience at age eleven. He's with us today because Jesus supernaturally kept him alive. David told me that, when he leads worship, he always goes back to that accident and connects with his pain. From his wounding flows a passion in worship that is contagious and lifegiving. He told me, "We were wounded by God so we would connect to our pain and live from that place."

When Jesus was pierced, a fountain was opened that gave life to the world. Similar things can happen through your piercing. That which wounded you can release life to your generation.

Either He wounds you, or the platform destroys you.

My friend psalmist Rita Springer has told me of sitting in a room with songwriters who are eager to come up with a good song, but they don't have the reservoir of a personal history with God to draw upon. She said something happens in you when you have to find the Presence through a haystack of hardship. She said, "I have grown most as a writer of worship in the corners of my wonder and worry."

Walk the ancient paths with Job, Jacob, Joseph, and Jeremiah. Yes, He wounds, but then He binds up (see Hosea 6:1). Wounded psalmists will inspire a generation to love Jesus through the turbulence of these end times.

This is the ancient way.

Fasting, Weeping, and Mourning

Any return to the ancient paths will include a return to fasting, weeping, and mourning. The Spirit's call through the prophet Joel rings clear as ever:

> *"Now, therefore," says the Lord, "Turn to Me with all your heart, with fasting, with weeping, and with mourning." So rend your heart, and not your garments; return to the Lord your God, for He is gracious and merciful, slow to anger, and of great kindness; and He relents from doing harm* (Joel 2:12–13).

As already stated, the only way forward, in the coming wave of worship, is through humility. When we humble ourselves before God in fasting and mourning, we receive the grace God gives the humble (see James 4:6).

Don't resist tears. They lubricate love, and they clear your eyes.

Mourning was a key element of the ancient psalmist anointing that rested on David. He expressed it in many of his psalms—what we call *laments*. Songs of lament access an ancient stream that can actually help us mount the coming waves of worship.

What should we mourn? Mourn the iniquities in your soul you can't change in your own strength (see Luke 18:13). Mourn your spiritual bankruptcy and blindness (see Rev. 3:17). Mourn your unbelief and hardness of heart (see Mark 16:14). Mourn the reproach that is on the Church of Jesus Christ in this hour (Zeph. 3:18).

How guttural does it get? Psalmist Chris Tofilon told me that he sometimes groans on his guitar. He said, "Sometimes I've vomited my emotions until I'm exhausted and don't want to talk to anyone."

Why do we mourn and weep? Because we believe Jesus' promise, *"Blessed are those who mourn, for they shall be comforted"* (Matt. 5:4).

How does He comfort us when we sorrow over our powerlessness? By releasing resurrection power to the Church.

How does He comfort our sorrow over our unbelief? By imparting mountain-moving faith. We mourn because we want His comfort!

The ancient grace of fasting will help us read the ocean and see how God is wanting to move in the Church today. I'm looking for a wave of worship that will capture resurrection power and see the fruit of mountain-moving faith!

Questions for Wave Riders:

1. How has God called you personally to ancient paths? Tell the group.

2. In what way have you experienced God's refining fire in your life?

3. Let's talk in our group about singing Scripture. Have you learned any keys that have helped you?

4. Choose a statement in this chapter you'd like the group to discuss.

5. How did you feel about the section on "Wounded Psalmists"? Does this concept produce fear or hope in you?

Note

1. I write about this in my book *The Cross: Never Too Dead for Resurrection.*

Chapter 14

COMING GLORY

A WAVE OF God's Glory is coming to the Church. Why do we know this? Because He said so. *"But truly, as I live, all the earth shall be filled with the glory of the Lord"* (Num. 14:21).

God promised at least three times in Scripture that His Glory would fill the earth (see Num. 14:21; Ps. 72:19; Hab. 2:14). The meaning in all three instances is that God is going to do something so significant, so powerful, and so supernatural that the entire earth will hear the report and affirm that *God did it!* In the coming wave of Glory, people around the world will acknowledge, "God has visited His people."

When Isaiah wrote about the coming Glory, he said, *"The glory of the Lord shall be revealed, and all flesh shall see it together; for the mouth of the Lord has spoken"* (Isa. 40:5).

Isaiah was speaking principally about John the Baptist and how he would prepare the way for Christ. When

Jesus launched His ministry, the Glory of the Lord was manifest through the many healings, signs, and wonders He performed. All flesh saw it together—that is, all the people present saw the bread and fish being multiplied. Everyone present saw the blind man healed and the dead son raised to life in his coffin. When Glory comes, everyone has the same objective experience, and they all see the same thing—together.

In the Presence realm, people receive subjective impressions and inner feelings; in the Glory realm, the spiritual realm literally breaks into the physical realm, and people see visible signs and wonders together.[1]

When God visits His Church with Glory, skeptics and unbelievers will see healings and signs just the same as believers. *"All flesh shall see it together."*

Get ready for Glory!

Great Gatherings

In the coming Glory wave, prepare for meetings that are thronged with people. I see this promised in verses such as these:

> *Behold, I will bring them from the north country, and gather them from the ends of the earth, among them the blind and the lame, the woman with child and the one who labors with child, together; a great throng shall return there* (Jeremiah 31:8).

"In that day," says the Lord, "I will assemble the lame, I will gather the outcast and those whom I have afflicted" (Micah 4:6).

The blind, lame, and infirm don't throng to large gatherings—because they don't fit. Their disabilities make them unwilling, in most cases, to participate in large crowds. But there's one exception—when Jesus is healing the sick. When the sound goes forth that God is visiting His people and the blind and lame are being healed, they will suddenly flock to the meetings. In the Glory realm, the wheelchairs will line up. They'll come confined to their wheelchairs and leave pushing their wheelchairs.

At the time of this writing, our churches have been emptied by COVID-19, and it's difficult to imagine people gathering en masse. But the Glory that's coming will be so explosive that the churches of the land will be unable to hold the harvest, and it will spill into the stadiums of the earth. Habakkuk prophesied, *"Before Him went pestilence"* (3:5). I wonder, therefore, if the Lord might use a pestilence like coronavirus to go before His face and prepare the Church for His visitation in signs and wonders.

Presence and Glory

The biblical connection between Presence and Glory is fascinating. They seem to be similar dynamics that reflect a spectrum of intensity. When God shows up at lesser levels of intensity, we experience His Presence; when

He shows up in greater levels of intensity, we experience His Glory.

Presence is a subjective, intangible encounter with Jesus in which everyone has their own personal experience with Him. Glory is an objective, visible encounter in which everyone sees the same thing and experiences Jesus in an objective, identifiable manner. Miracles and healings, for example, are part of the Glory realm.

The Church was born in Glory in the upper room, which means you have Glory in your DNA (see Acts 2). You love the Presence of Jesus, but you'll never be satisfied until you're experiencing Glory. Presence is the earmark of the Church, and Glory is the vindication of the Church (see Exod. 33:16; Eph. 3:21).

Reaching for Glory

What can we do to touch waves of Glory? Let me suggest three things.

First, get into His Presence, and then contend for more. The Presence realm is available to all of us, all the time. When you meet, even with just two or three, Jesus is present with you (see Matt. 18:20). Get in His Presence, linger there, and gently push in the Spirit for more. Churches are being planted these days on this priority. They're Presence churches. Their purpose is to gather in His Presence, minister to Him, and watch to see what He wants to do. When you honor His Presence, you're positioned for Glory.

Let me use a different metaphor to illustrate this first point. When Jesus visited a certain house to raise a young girl who had died, He said, *"Make room, for the girl is not dead, but sleeping"* (Matt. 9:24). The room had to be cleared of the clutter before Jesus could show His Glory and raise her from the dead. *You have to make room for resurrection.* Create space, therefore, for Jesus to demonstrate His Glory. We can do that by getting in His Presence, ministering to Him, waiting on Him, and pressing for more.

Second, sow to the Spirit. I have Hosea 8:7 in view, *"They sow the wind, and reap the whirlwind."* In context, Hosea is speaking of the Israelites who practiced idolatry. When they worshiped false gods, they were sowing to the wind and would ultimately reap a whirlwind of judgment. But I reckon the opposite must also be true. When we're worshiping Jesus, we're sowing to the winds of the Spirit. Is it possible that, if we'll sow to the winds of the Spirit, we may eventually reap a whirlwind of Glory (see Job 38:1; Ezek. 1:4)?

Third, ask. If you want to experience waves of Glory, ask for it. Moses is our model, who asked of the Lord, *"Please, show me Your Glory"* (Exod. 33:18). God's response was basically, "I show My Glory to whomever I want, whenever I want. And I've decided to say *yes* to you." And then God encountered Moses with His trifecta of

Glory—the same trifecta experienced by Ezekiel, Isaiah, Jacob, and John.

What's the trifecta of Glory? An encounter with God in which you *see* something, you *hear* something, and you *feel* something supernatural. Moses saw the Lord, heard His voice, and then the Lord placed His hand over Moses. It was Glory! To experience such Glory, sometimes all you can do is ask and then see what He says.

When Jesus visits His Church in Glory, worship leaders, get ready for a wild surf!

Questions for Wave Riders:

1. When Glory comes, everyone has the same objective experience together. Do you have a story to tell of experiencing this?

2. *You love the Presence of Jesus, but you'll never be satisfied until you're experiencing Glory.* In what way do you resonate with that statement?

3. What does making room for Glory mean to you?

4. Would you want to pray together as a group—*Lord, please show us Your Glory?*

Note

1. I expand on this glorious topic in my book *Glory: When Heaven Invades Earth.*

Chapter 15

HOW TO CATCH THE WAVE

IN THIS BOOK, we've used the metaphor of surfing to illustrate how worship ministries seek to catch the waves of the Holy Spirit in worship. By now, I hope your appetite has been aroused to go surfing. I can imagine a worship leader asking, "What's something practical we can do to become more adept at reading the ocean of the Spirit's movements and capturing what He's doing in the moment?"

I'll suggest three things. Here's my first piece of advice: Expect the unexpected.

Expect the Unexpected

When you follow the ministry of Jesus in the Gospels, you're struck with how unexpected everything was that He did. His teachings were unexpected, astonishing the crowds (see Matt. 7:28). His miracles were unexpected, wowing the people (see Mark 2:12). For the disciples,

145

following Jesus was an adventure of new surprises every day. His words, responses, initiatives, and perspectives were all continuously unexpected.

When we come to the most vibrant worship service in Jesus' ministry, it's marked by—you guessed it—the unexpected. I have the triumphal entry in view. The praise that ignited during the triumphal entry was unprecedented and unmatched, in Jesus' three years of ministry, for its vibrancy, energy, volume, and crowd momentum.

For three years, Jesus repeatedly told His followers, "Don't tell anyone!" But now, when He mounted the colt, headed for Jerusalem, and the crowds began to praise, Jesus' countenance was giving them permission to shout it out. Under His nodding approval, they vented the praises that had been bottled up in their hearts and lifted their cries of, "Hosanna!"

His critics asked Him to rebuke the praisers, which prompted Him to say, *"I tell you that if these should keep silent, the stones would immediately cry out"* (Luke 19:40). Luke explained why the praises were so exuberant. He said the whole multitude rejoiced and praised God *"with a loud voice for all the mighty works they had seen"* (19:37). Three years of wonder at Jesus' works were pent up in these people. Realizing that Jesus was smiling, the dam of praise broke open and burst forth with loud shouts of acclamation!

But then Jesus did the unexpected: He began to weep over Jerusalem (see Luke 19:41). Right in the middle of the praise service! I can imagine the disciples thinking, *Jesus, what are You doing? For once we actually have a good, old-fashioned, Davidic-style praise service. Why are you weeping? You're throwing a damper on the momentum of the meeting. We're having the praise party of the decade, and You're getting all sorrowful. If we're to keep this praise service going, we need You to cooperate a little, Lord. This is a time for joy, not tears!*

But for Jesus, it was suddenly a time for tears as He prophesied over the city:

> *If you had known, even you, especially in this your day, the things that make for your peace! But now they are hidden from your eyes. For days will come upon you when your enemies will build an embankment around you, surround you and close you in on every side, and level you, and your children within you, to the ground; and they will not leave in you one stone upon another, because you did not know the time of your visitation* (Luke 19:42–44).

When the disciples looked on this new face of Jesus, they didn't know what to do. "He's like . . . He's weeping, I mean, what do we do now, guys?" They were feeling the uncertainty of the unexpected.

Several elements surrounding this explosive worship event were surprises:

- They never expected Jesus to mount an untrained colt.

- They didn't expect Him to allow such extravagant, public praise.

- They didn't expect the stones would be on standby if they stopped crying out.

- They didn't expect Jesus to start weeping right in the middle of the praise march—just when it was starting to capture the attention of Jerusalem.

- They didn't expect Him to drive out of the temple those who bought and sold.

- They didn't expect Him to curse a fig tree simply because it wasn't producing ripe figs out of season.

If *that* worship service was marked by the unexpected, then get ready for *your* worship services also to be caught off balance by the unexpected. Because when Jesus is in the house, anything can happen!

The next waves of worship will be:

- unexpected in their timing.

- unexpected in the direction they come from.

- unexpected in the way they form, turn, change, and break.

- unexpected by some who mount it and some who miss it.
- unexpected in their intensity.
- unexpected in their message and focus.

At the triumphal entry, there was only one way to realize that the movements of worship had changed: The people had to keep their eyes riveted on Jesus. Only by gazing on His countenance could they follow the movements of the wave.

How will we follow the waves of the Holy Spirit in worship today? The same way—by keeping our eyes fixed on Jesus.

In the coming decades, Jesus is going to be taking us places in worship we never anticipated. Therefore, let me say it again: *Keep your eyes on Him, and expect the unexpected.*

Here's my second piece of advice: Watch for altars God honors.

Altars God Honors

One way to learn how to read the ocean of the Spirit's movements is to watch for altars God likes. When I say that, I'm thinking of a time in David's life when he took special note of an altar God honored (see 1 Chron. 21). Let me review the story.

Satan tempted David to measure the strength of his military, and succumbing to pride, David fell for it. He decided to count the number of warriors in his army. The Lord was displeased and gave David three choices of punishment for his error: three years of famine, three months of military defeat, or three days of God's sword. David chose the Lord's sword to be against him because of his confidence in the Lord's mercies. In response, the Lord sent a destroying angel that killed 70,000 Israelites with a pandemic (a plague) in three days.

We might wonder why God was so displeased with David for numbering his army. Perhaps it was because God had proven repeatedly to David that his military victories were not because of the strength of his army, but because God fought for him. Was David now going to number his warriors as though the size of his army would be his source of deliverance? Consequently, the size of David's army was significantly reduced in a stern rebuke.

Ornan was a Jebusite who lived in Jerusalem at the time. As the destroying angel approached Ornan's property, the Lord commanded the angel to stop the destruction. It was enough. Then the Lord instructed David to erect an altar of sacrifice at Ornan's threshing floor where the angel had stopped. Here's what happened:

> *And David built there an altar to the Lord, and offered burnt offerings and peace offerings, and called on the Lord; and He answered him from heaven by fire on the altar of burnt offering* (1 Chronicles 21:26).

This is the only record we have of God sending fire down on an altar David had made. When heavenly fire fell on that altar, David paid attention. He observed that, for some reason, God liked the altar. He realized there was something about this altar that was bigger than the moment. God was placing a marker on that specific location. Yes, He was providing mercy for David's sin, but even more than that, He was establishing a place where mercy would be released to the nation for many generations to come.

In response, David said, *"This is the house of the Lord God, and this is the altar of burnt offering for Israel"* (1 Chron. 22:1). Connecting the dots, he discerned that the Lord's house was to be built at that very location. And sure enough, it became the site for Solomon's temple.

David was able to partner with God's plans because he was attentive to an altar God honored.

Here's what David's example teaches us: Watch for altars God likes—that is, moments in worship when the fire of God falls. When you see God honoring a worship context with uncommon Holy Spirit activity, pay attention because He's communicating. He's showing you there was something about that altar that moved His heart in a special way. When you're alert in those moments, you'll learn things about the waves of the Spirit in worship.

Let me tell another story to illustrate this point. On one occasion, I was invited to speak to an inter-church gathering of worship ministries in a certain city. The worship team for the event was selected from several churches. Specifically, the drummer, keyboardist, guitarist, and bass guitarist were from four different churches. All the musicians and singers were of exceptional musical caliber but had never ministered together in that particular configuration before.

The worship team wanted to get together to rehearse and prepare for the workshop, but the event organizer wouldn't allow it. In fact, he actually prohibited them from practicing their set list in advance. They could get together to pray and to share in fellowship, but not to rehearse musically.

As it turned out, the brother who was chosen to lead the worship set took sick at the last minute and had to stay home. Leadership of the worship set fell to the backup worship leader—a sister in the Lord who is a dear, personal friend of mine.

I arrived to the workshop a bit early and learned that my friend was suddenly being tapped to lead worship that morning. This change was a surprise, and when this new expectation was suddenly placed on her, she wanted to hold a quick rehearsal with the musicians before the meeting started. But the event organizer held his ground and wouldn't allow it.

My friend was frustrated that she wasn't permitted to rehearse with the team. I was aware of her frustration because I happened to overhear her expressing her frustration to her husband. She wanted to do a quick rehearsal, and the organizer wouldn't allow it!

When the event kicked off at nine that morning, I was watching with a little bit of curiosity because I was now aware that there was frustration on the platform. I was curious to see how it was all going to pan out.

What I'm about to describe is without exaggeration. The moment the worship team sang the first line of the first song, Jesus walked into the room. I wasn't the only one to sense it. I think virtually everyone in the room was aware that the Lord was with us in an uncommon way. We went from the earthly to the heavenly in about three seconds.

In that moment, all of the worship leader's apprehensions vaporized instantly. Jesus was with us! We knew it was going to be a glorious time of worship because, when Jesus is in the room, it hardly matters what songs you sing or how polished your musical sound. And sure enough, we had a marvelous time together in the Lord's Presence.

I realized, *God likes this altar.* I found myself wondering, *What is it about this worship altar that is pleasing to Him?* I'm not sure I read the moment perfectly, but it seemed to me that God was pleased with our refusal to lean on the strengths of human musicianship. It would have been so easy to do, because all the musicians on the platform were so excellent at their craft. In my mind, a little bit of rehearsal would have made them all the more cohesive musically. But instead, they restrained themselves from polish and finesse. In place of strength, they chose weakness. In place of confidence, they chose uncertainty. From my window, it seemed to me that, when they chose not to lean on human means, they opened to divine impetus.

Maybe He liked that the altar was earthen, not chiseled.

Now, let me be clear. I'm not saying that the Lord doesn't want worship ministries to rehearse. I've already pointed out in this book the essential nature of preparation. But there comes a time when He wants us to cease polishing our natural strengths and set our focus on partnering with the Holy Spirit's movements.

God might surprise you with the altars He honors. If He sends fire at a moment you weren't expecting, see what you can learn from it. Our focus isn't on finding altars *we* like but that *He* likes.

To participate in the coming Glory, pay attention to the altars God honors—that is, worship services in which His Presence is manifest in an unusually strong way. If you do, you'll learn how to read the ocean and anticipate the waves the Holy Spirit wants to honor.

And here's my final piece of practical advice: Serve God with your spirit.

Serve God with Your Spirit

In writing to the church at Rome, Paul said, *"For God is my witness, whom I serve with my spirit in the gospel of His Son, that without ceasing I make mention of you always in my prayers"* (Rom. 1:9). I want to highlight his phrase, "whom I serve with my spirit."

Paul was exceptionally strong in his soul and mind. I would call him *a five-talent guy.* When I say that, I'm remembering the parable in Matthew 25 in which Jesus said that one person was given five talents, another two, and another one. On the spectrum of one to five, Paul was a five. In other words, he was an impressive package of gifts and strengths. He was a brilliant thinker, a tender feeler, a compelling communicator, a winsome leader, a systems builder, a bold risk-taker, and a capable disciple-maker, to name just a few of his many gifts.

But he didn't say he served God with his talents or with his gifts, strengths, or abilities. He said he served God with his *spirit.* Although he would have been tempted to depend on his many talents and gifts, Paul intentionally devoted himself to serving God with his spirit.

Similar to Paul, musicians and worship leaders are some of the most gifted people you'll ever meet. It's because of their multi-gift set that they're able to learn a musical instrument, master chord structure and chord progressions, understand chordal voicings, play an instrument while singing, lead an entire worship department, write songs, learn the latest worship hits, lead in a variety of musical genres, sense the temperature of the congregation, follow the leading of the Holy Spirit, stay on pitch, and do it all from a highly visible platform.

But here's the weakness of five-talent people: They tend to rely on their talents. It's their common temptation. When your gift set is strong, it's tempting to leverage your strengths and muscle your way forward, rather than slowing down and going deep with Jesus in the secret place.

But natural gifts and talents have a ceiling—that is, they can only go so far. They're limited in accomplishing eternal Kingdom purposes. To fulfill your upward calling, you must learn to serve God with your spirit.

Good news: You need not be limited to your gifts and talents. When you function within the limits of your skill set, your impact will be small and your sphere parochial. But you don't have to be limited to your skill set. I don't care how many talents you have, whether five, two, or one, you need not be limited to your talents. God wants to lift you onto waves of the Spirit that go far beyond your gifts and natural abilities.

You need not be limited to your talents. I want to illustrate that truth with a five-talent guy and a one-talent gal. First, our five-talent guy.

Joseph

Joseph was a five-talent guy—he had stuff cooking on every burner. He had people skills, brain power, strong physique, business acumen, leadership abilities, charisma, and more. Everything he touched turned to gold. If God had left him alone, he would have gone through life depending on his talents and gifts. But God had a realm of influence and impact for Joseph that exceeded his five talents. He was good, but not good enough. To steward the sphere God was giving him, Joseph would need to find something much stronger and deeper than his talents.

How could he find a deeper dimension in God? Prison. God put Joseph in prison and shut down all his talents. Joseph found himself in a prison where every gift he had cultivated as a steward in Potiphar's house was now rendered useless. His people skills and business skills would never get him out of prison. How would he ever get out of prison? Joseph was desperate to know.

Prison left Joseph with only one option: Lay hold of God! He was forced to push down roots into God deeper than he ever had to before. It was Joseph's depth in God that changed everything. He eventually got out of prison—not because he exercised his talents, but because he found a dimension in God that is, *"Not by might nor by power, but by My Spirit,' says the Lord of hosts"* (Zech. 4:6).

Joseph's depth in the Holy Spirit enabled him to do far more than his talents would have ever accomplished. He was enabled to save the lives of all the people of Egypt, to become a feeder of nations, and to establish his family in prosperity in the land of Goshen. He rose far beyond his five talents because he tapped into the reserves of the Holy Spirit.

To every five-talent musician out there, I want to say: *You need not be limited to your talents*. Pursue a depth of relationship with God, and your inheritance in the Kingdom will be much greater than your five talents could ever touch.

I'm illustrating this principle: *You need not be limited to your talents*. For another example, let me talk about a one-talent gal in the Bible.

Anna

I reckon Anna was probably a one-talent woman. From the biblical account, we get no indication she was highly educated or refined. She was the kind of woman who probably thought, *There's one thing I can do well. I can be a good wife and mother.*

But seven years into her marriage, God took the life of her husband and removed from her the ability to exercise the one talent she had. Widowhood plummeted her into the abyss of her life. I can imagine her saying, "God, I don't get You. I've loved You, served You, walked blamelessly before You, and now You've taken away from me everything I've ever longed for." The Lord's answer simply seemed to be, "Anna, go deeper."

Anna probably went on, "But, God, I don't understand You. I've followed You in faithfulness and obedience, and I've only asked one thing of You. And the one thing I've ever asked of You—to be a wife and mother—You've taken away. Who are You, anyway?" And all the Lord seemed to say was, "Deeper. Go deeper."

In the desperation of her sorrow, Anna began to push roots into God deeper than ever before. She went into fasting and prayer, and stationed herself in the temple in prayers and intercessions. Then one day I believe she heard another word from God: "Messiah."

Anna was like, *Messiah? Is that what this is about?* Her intercession deepened, and she went into labor in her prayers like someone who was giving birth.

Through her intercessory ministry, Anna actually *prayed in the Messiah*. Eventually, she held in her arms the fruit of her intercessory travail. A one-talent woman who thought her motherhood had been stolen from her became *a mother to millions*. Why? Because she found a dimension in the Spirit that went beyond her one talent, that is *"'Not by might nor by power, but by My Spirit,' says the Lord of hosts"* (Zech. 4:6).

I want to say to every one-talent reader: *You need not be limited to your talent.* Pursue the heart of God, go deep in the Spirit, and He can do more through your life than your talent would ever allow.

Go Deep in the Spirit

Where God is taking us in worship can't be fully discovered through our strengths and talents. Why not? Because we'll find it, not through our talents, but through the power of the Spirit. The greatest Kingdom exploits will be accomplished when our spirit connects with His Spirit. To enter this dimension, we must *serve God with our spirit*.

I've found it helpful to locate my spirit. In John 7:38, Jesus spoke of our spirit as being activated in the region of our *belly*. The seat of the human spirit, therefore, is in the vicinity of the gut. To connect with your spirit, don't go to your head, and don't go to your heart. Go deeper, to your gut—the area of your solar plexus. Serve God from *there*.

Play your keyboard from your spirit. Play your guitar from your spirit. Play the drums from your spirit. Play the bass guitar from your spirit. Play your wind instrument from your spirit. Sing alto or tenor from your spirit. Sing prophetic oracles from your spirit.

The Lord has helped you to learn how to serve Him with your instrument and voice. Now, ask Him to teach you how to serve Him with your spirit. He's eager to train you, and He's waiting for you to ask.

He'll teach you to read the ocean, discern the sweet spot in the Spirit's waves, and rise on the crest of the Holy Spirit's movements in the midst of the Church. As you serve God with your spirit, the name of Jesus will be lifted high to the glory of the Father, and the Church will be enabled to make herself ready for the return of her beloved Savior.

Even so, Lord Jesus, come!

Questions for Wave Riders:

1. When everyone at the triumphal entry was lifting shouts of joy, Jesus was weeping. What have you learned from this story?

2. Have you ever experienced an unusual altar where the fire of God fell in a meeting? What did you learn from the experience?

3. What does it mean to you to serve God with your spirit? What do you sense God speaking to you about serving Him in worship with your spirit?

4. Have you had a prison experience where God did a deep work in you? In what way did that change how you view restriction and confinement?

5. What is the most valuable thing you're taking with you from your reading in this book?

Chapter 16

GET READY TO RIDE

IN THIS NEW era, we're preparing ourselves for the next wave of worship the Holy Spirit is sending. Throughout this book, we've looked at how we can become better students of His ways—because we want to partner with Him in the coming waves of Glory. Allow me to review some of those highlights.

We took several chapters to review how God has been growing the worship movement over the past sixty years. We're riding today on the crest of a worship movement that has been building and developing for decades. When we pause to look back, often the way forward becomes clearer. God gave us gifts in yesterday's worship that will empower and facilitate tomorrow's worship.

We celebrate what the Church's worship looks like today, and yet we want to keep progressing. If you feel we're a bit stuck today in playlist worship, you're not alone. In playlist worship, the people in the room have the same experience as those watching the livestream.

I've tried to show how we're back in a 1960s model of four songs on Sunday morning. But God never meant for worship to be a playlist. Corporate worship is a vital, organic, living, romantic dance between Bridegroom and Bride. Let's not tether the Breath to a playlist.

There's something present about Presence. To experience His Presence, we must be present.

We want His Presence to be so real that we'll say to those who watched the webstream, "You missed it!" Presence worship is the wave of the future.

Surfing is the primary metaphor of this book. We learned that if you want to catch a wave, you must be positioned for it. You don't learn anything about surfing until you get in the water. When you're in the water, then you can learn to read the ocean of God's movements in the earth. To read the ocean, you must keep your gaze on the countenance of Christ.

God's Presence isn't moved by mechanical things but by living things. The Philistine cart David attempted to use represents human means to move God's Presence in corporate worship. The next wave will be empowered, not by human means, but heavenly impetus.

Worship isn't chiseled but earthy.

The Levites carried the Presence on their shoulders to help us see that leading worship is rigorous. Worship leaders are shepherds who take worshipers on a journey into the heart of God. There are people in the room who will connect with God based on how we shoulder the moment. Sometimes we have to slow down so we can catch up with Jesus.

One of the primary objectives of worship ministries is to release the song of the people. In the next wave, the skill of worship leaders will be measured, not by their musical excellence, but their ability to unlock the song of the people. We're not trying to start a bonfire on the platform but a forest fire in the congregation.

One reason we've lost the song of the people is because we allowed the 1970s gift of singing in the Spirit to fall into disrepair. We'll do well to go back and recover the gracious gifts God gave the worship movement in the 1970s and 80s. We want watchers to become worshipers. Once again, we must teach God's people to sing past the song.

What will release the song of the people? Historic revivals are one of the primary means God has used to restore the song of the people. God is going to send a revival with signs and wonders, and we're going to see a resurgence of the song of the people. The joyful sound of Psalm 89:15 is the sound of praise that will erupt in the next wave when God demonstrates His power in signs, wonders, miracles, and healing.

I've shown how the Lamb of God is the center of all worship. The next wave of worship will be cross-centric. The cross is the fountainhead of all worship, and Jesus placed the Lord's Supper at the center of our worship. We'll pursue the new innovations of worship, therefore, by clinging tenaciously to the ancient cross of Christ. You can't discern the new unless you're living in the ancient.

A wave is coming in which worship ministries will be released to do more than just sing songs. Entire congregations are going to sing Scripture together. Our worship expressions will become more equally distributed between psalms, hymns, and spiritual songs. We're going to explore the glories of spontaneous worship—which is the freedom to move seamlessly between psalms, hymns, and spiritual songs.

The more spontaneous you want to be, the more you must prepare.

I used the metaphor of a kite to show that the deeper you go in truth, the higher you can soar in the Spirit.

We examined the ancient psalmist anointing that was on David. That psalmist anointing is cultivated through Word immersion. Singing Scripture is the ancient way of the psalmists. A psalmist's strongest anointing is not on a platform but in the secret place.

Worship leaders, either He wounds you, or the platform destroys you. Never despise your tears. They lubricate love and clear your eyes.

I dedicated a chapter to the coming Glory. You love His Presence, but you'll never be satisfied until you're experiencing Glory. You have to make room for Glory.

Watch for the unexpected, and learn from the worship altars God honors. And finally, serve God with your spirit.

I wanted to summarize these highlights to help you carry the message of this book into this next decade. It's a new era of worship, and God is choosing young psalmists who will learn to read the ocean and ride the waves of the Spirit's movements in these last days. Those who adopt a John the Baptist lifestyle will be privileged to see the Dove and identify what He's doing.

The next wave is coming—get ready to ride!

ABOUT BOB SORGE

Bob is best known for his popular devotional book, *Secrets of the Secret Place*. Find his books at your favorite retailer, through all the eBook channels, and Audible. To stay current on Bob's writing and traveling ministry, connect with him here:

YouTube.com/bobsorge

Instagram: bob.sorge

Site: www.oasishouse.com

Blog: bobsorge.com

twitter.com/BOBSORGE

Facebook.com/BobSorgeMinistry